Praise for *Evolving*

"In the world of science, accumulating data leads to the adjustment of theories. In law, accumulating evidence leads to the overturning of convictions. In religion, it often takes a hard, long struggle to adjust or overturn long-held beliefs. But when it happens, the change usually comes through accumulating stories. I am grateful that Susanne Bennett has shown the courage and care to tell hers, late in her seventies. It is beautifully written and rings with authenticity."

—Brian D. McLaren, PhD
Author of *Faith After Doubt*

"Dr. C. Susanne Bennett has written a powerful, inspiring, and engaging memoir. Through carefully curated personal events at various stages of her life, she describes the unfolding of the intersecting and fluid nature of her faith and sexuality in the context of social and political turmoil over the course of seven decades. Her curiosity, openness, and self-reflection reveal a journey to self-understanding as a person who is wholly beloved by God. This memoir is dotted with insights from child development theories and spiritual wisdom that ground her personal experiences in long-studied disciplines. The book also includes a set of thoughtful reflection questions that can be used in book clubs or classrooms. This memoir is an important book for this time and one that generously offers a rare insight into an expansive process of aging, faith, and sexuality."

—Linda Plitt Donaldson, MSW, PhD
Associate Dean of the College of Health & Behavioral Sciences
James Madison University, Harrisonburg, VA

"*Evolving* is such a well-written, thoughtful memoir—and so, so needed. The two threads of faith and sexuality intertwine beautifully, and are anchored by Dr. Bennett's expertise and grounded voice. She's truly harvested her experiences to show how she's evolved in her beliefs. This book is a wonderful teaching tool for individuals and for groups. What an absolute gift to offer the world!"

—Caitlin Elizabeth
Editor and Author

"At this time of much seeking and confusion in both faith and sexuality, Susanne Bennett's heartfelt memoir arrives to guide us through a lifetime of inquisitive and intentional transitions. Susanne brings her pressing personal questions into her studies and academic career, offering fresh insight to both spiritual growth and sexual dynamics. Through tumultuous times of social change including our own, Susanne's deep trust in her authentic self invites and inspires us each to find our own true path."

—Sherry Cassedy, JD
Author of *Marriage Unveiled*

"Rarely are the two words sexuality and spirituality found together, but Dr. Bennett has wisely found a way to integrate them and demonstrate how they live and grow together in her own life. So much of Western religious thought has sought to separate these energies. It is time for them to be seen as integral and natural aspects of healthy spirituality. I especially found the Appendix questions helpful as I looked at my own life and growth."

—The Rev. Carlyle Gill
Episcopal Priest and Spiritual Director

"Dr. Bennett has offered us an autobiography that provides unique insight into the complexity and mystery of sexuality. This illuminating story is interwoven with her faith struggles and development growing up Southern Baptist with a father who was a seminary professor and dean (my dean at one time) at a prominent seminary, along with her own expertise as a researcher, professor, and therapist. She structures her story around Brian McLaren's stages of faith development from simplicity to complexity to perplexity to harmony. The dynamism of her personal story is complemented by insights from her professional background and her faith journey. Along the way, she offers confusion, pain, affirmation, wisdom, love, and also humor. In addition to its readability, the questions and meditations for each chapter are helpful, making the book very easily used by a reading group. As the subtitle indicates, Bennett's life story offers a captivating account of faith, sexuality, and aging that contributes to the much-needed understanding of the full range of human experience."

—Dan R. Stiver, MDiv, PhD
President and Professor of Theology
Jesse C. Fletcher Seminary, San Antonio, TX

Evolving

Evolving

Faith, Sexuality, and Aging

C. Susanne Bennett

SOUTHERN STONEHENGE PRESS
2025

—

Published in North America.

This is a work of memoir, and while based on true events, some names and identifying details have been changed to protect the privacy of individuals involved. The author has tried to faithfully recount experiences as remembered, but some events may have been compressed or rearranged for narrative purposes.

.

Paperback ISBN: 979-8-218-61668-7

First print edition: 2025

In memory of

G. Willis Bennett (1919-1994)
& Caroline D. Bennett (1921-1995)

my original secure base & safe haven

Contents

Preface

This memoir explores the intersection of my evolving faith and sexuality over nearly eight decades, set against the backdrop of an era marked by intense debates and divisions about sexuality, gender, race, and religion. I was motivated to write this book within the context of these cultural debates, from the unique perspective of my life journey, my education, my life of faith, and my embrace of diversity. My stories explore how the arc of my psychosocial and spiritual development—shaped by my questions and doubts—helped me understand my sense of self and life changes. My doctoral studies at a college in New England focused on cultural studies related to diversity and psychological theories concerning self, attachment, human development, and change. These academic studies and contemporary cultural issues significantly influenced my writing.

My writing began with a gift from my daughter, who gave me Storyworth, a software program that chronicled my life stories as I wrote them online. She posed weekly questions, and I responded with written memories from early childhood to the present day. Essentially, she inquired about those things she wanted to know but had never asked. Some questions were fun but superficial: "What fads did you embrace growing up?" Others were more thought-provoking: "What brings meaning for you at this stage of life?" After a year of writing, the program turned my 43 life stories into a 400-page hardbound book with pictures to share with my two adult children and grandchildren.

Writing these stories was integrating, like putting together jigsaw puzzle pieces of my life and seeing the bigger picture of who I am. The primary benefit of my year of reminiscence was the opportunity to examine my life's most significant moments and themes. As I wrote my life stories, two major themes emerged: how my faith evolved over my lifetime and how my sexuality changed in ways I could never have imagined. I began to see how these themes are linked, and their coming together brings me to a place of knowing my true self. For your reflection or even group discussion, at the end of this memoir, I have included a section with reflection questions to spark your thoughts, just as the weekly questions from my daughter prompted my initial reminiscences.

When I told my adult son the proposed title of this memoir, he immediately said somewhat teasingly, "Wow, Mom! That should be a best-seller! It's about everything people are most uncomfortable discussing—faith, sex, and old age!" I laughed spontaneously and saw his point. Nevertheless, I hope my stories about the intersection of my evolving faith and fluid sexuality spark curiosity, challenge beliefs, provoke questions and doubts, and assure those whose life stories may resonate with mine.

Susanne Bennett
2025

Introduction

_____

Stages and Themes

Many friends have told me, "You should write a book about your unusual life! It's quite a story!" My life began as a child raised in the South where my faith was chosen for me. As I moved from girlhood into adolescence, college, and young adulthood, my faith evolved, moving away from the religious teachings I absorbed at my father's knee. This evolution of my faith continued throughout my life, shaped by the questions or doubts I confronted. As I moved from young adulthood, to middle age, and now late adulthood, my understanding of sexuality and gender also changed. Reflecting on my evolving faith and fluid sexuality, I have come to see how these foundational life themes intersect and share similarities. Altogether, they form the core of this memoir and who I am.

I often modeled my search for meaning after my father, a man of faith who spent his life serving others as an ordained Baptist minister and seminary professor, committed to the church's involvement in the community and the world. He generally welcomed my questions and supported my search for answers through education. As an educator, researcher, and clinician, when I find myself in doubt or turmoil, I turn to wiser voices than mine to try to understand what I am experiencing. I find comfort in learning about what others have confronted, their similar questions, and their experiences. I study and examine their ideas against my own experiences to help me navigate and integrate my circumstances. My search for wiser voices about my faith journey led me to Brian McLaren, an author, activist, and public theologian.

In his 2021 book *Faith After Doubt*,[1] McLaren explores how faith evolves through questions that evoke doubts about our assumptions and belief systems regarding our lives and the world. Doubts about faith may come as the human brain matures, such as when children and adolescents develop critical thinking skills and question what they were taught at a younger age. As they mature, children see the world more skeptically, losing their belief in magic and miracles. Doubts may also emerge when significant losses, such as the end of a marriage, the death of a loved one, or a critical health crisis, shake our foundation of faith. We ask how there can be a God when such a tragedy or trauma occurs. McLaren proposes four stages of faith development, which he calls simplicity, complexity, perplexity, and harmony. He suggests that "doubt is the passageway from one stage to the next... Growth from one stage to another usually requires us to doubt the assumptions that give shape to our current stage."[2] He proposes that when our worldview is shaken, creating confusion, crisis, and loneliness, we are at an opening to a new stage.

McLaren's stages of faith strongly resonate with me because my faith development aligns with his four-stage schema. When I first read his book, I felt he used my life experiences to describe his stages. His stages relate to my childhood faith of simplicity, my adolescent and young adult faith of complexity, my post-divorce faith of perplexity, and my current retirement faith of harmony. Reflecting on my life transitions, this theory helped me embrace the importance of doubt in my developing faith.

My life story has also been notably shaped by my fluid sexuality, which is the second major theme in my life. To my surprise, in middle age, my own sexual attraction and responsiveness changed, influenced by my family history and an erotic relationship I developed with a female friend. The eventual transition of my sexual orientation from men to women was complicated by my childhood religious upbringing, causing me to question both my faith and my sexuality and leading me to wonder what my "true self" was. I found affirmation in the research of psychologist Lisa Diamond, who has found that sexual fluidity is common among women, more so than men, and is a "normal" sexual response "that can occur in any woman at any age in life."[3] Diamond also says: "Women of all orientations may experience variation in their erotic and affectional feelings as they encounter different situations, relationships, and life stages."[4]

3

As these changes took place in my own life, I dedicated myself to obtaining a doctoral degree in social work, focusing my studies on attachment and relationships within gay families. Combined with my earlier university studies in religion and theology and my current training in contemplative spirituality and spiritual direction, I began to understand how my faith and sexuality intersect. As I matured, my perspectives on sexuality, sexual orientation, and gender evolved, as did the evolution of my faith.

There were times when my faith made me question how to navigate sexual situations. When I was a young adolescent with a simple faith, for example, my high school boyfriend wanted me to go back on the pledge I made in church, where I promised not to have sex before marriage. There were other times when my sexuality served as a gateway to the next stage of my faith development, such as when I married my wife. Our relationship and love for each other led me into a faith stage of harmony. In other words, my evolving faith and my sexuality were often intertwined, mutually influencing each other.

This memoir reflects these significant changes in my life. Similarly, this story shares how my sexuality has also transitioned from one of simplicity to complexity to perplexity and, finally, harmony. From the perspective today of my late adulthood and a long-term marriage with my wife, I recognize that both faith and sexuality are dynamic, evolving aspects of my true self. They intersect and influence who I am, assuring me that God loves me just

4

as I am. I hope my unique story will inspire self-acceptance in others who embrace diversity and a life of faith.

Part One

Childhood and Adolescence

One

Childhood Simplicity

Your life is already a miracle of chance

Waiting for you to shape its destiny.

—*Toni Morrison*[1]

I grew up a Southern Baptist preacher's kid, a "PK," raised in a traditional, religious, white, middle-class family in the segregated South of the 1950s. PKs had the reputation in those days of being either "very good" or "very bad." As a little girl, I fit the very good version, attending church without fuss whenever the doors opened, learning my Bible verses, and saying my prayers. My father, Willis Bennett, was the minister of our church when I was a child. I grew up sitting in the pews with my mother and sisters, hearing him preach every Sunday morning.

There was nothing near the intersection of the two rural roads where I lived as a young child except the large brick church up on the hill and the church parsonage, a house provided for the pastor's family. This home where my family and I lived was across the road from the church. I played with the little girl from the tobacco farm a few miles away, often swimming in her pond, where we had to watch out for water moccasins. But I mainly saw my friends in church and Sunday school. The Olive Chapel Baptist Church was the heart of this rural community in the Piedmont area of North Carolina, about 20 miles from Raleigh, the state capitol. Because Dad was the minister, my family and friends were involved in every activity the church offered.

I firmly believed the Bible stories my parents and Sunday school teachers taught me that God lives in heaven above the earth, and his son Jesus came down from heaven to save me from my sins. If I believed Jesus was God's son and tried to model my life after his, I would "have eternal life." We drove down our country roads and saw the words "John 3:16" plastered on billboards and barn sides. I never once questioned those famous words, which I still know by heart:

> For God so loved the world that he gave his only begotten Son, that whoever believes in him should not perish but have eternal life. —John 3:16, RSV

This Christian mantra formed the basis of my seven-year-old profession of faith. I believed that "God is love" and that "Jesus loves me," just as my Bible verses taught me.

I felt genuinely loved by my parents and God, not just because I believed my Bible verses but because of how our family lived. My extroverted mom was warm and affectionate, bringing life and joy to our family of five. My more serious-minded dad was the family explainer. Dad was intellectual but also nurturing and empathic. Mom was the one who made us laugh and made Dad's eyes twinkle, but Dad was the one who made me feel secure. He was a safe and steady presence, ready to allay my fears and answer my questions. He would assure me when I was scared.

When I was five, my younger sister and I shared a bedroom on the second floor while our baby sister slept in a crib down the hall. In the days before air conditioning overcame Southern heat, a 6-foot-wide exhaust fan was built into the parsonage attic, a common addition to many Southern homes. This large, rattling fan sucked out the daytime heat of our sweltering small, brick house and brought in cooler, humid air at night. On hot summer evenings when the fan was in full operation, the sound made me worry that something scary lived upstairs. I was afraid to go up to my room alone because it was noisy and dark, and something might jump out at me. Dad would kindly take my hand, walk me up the stairs, and calmly explain about the noisy fan. Then, together, we would check under the bed and in the closet for the boogeyman until I felt safe and my heart rate returned to normal. After my sister and I said our bedtime prayers, Dad would always sit with us until we fell asleep.

My dad spent long hours explaining God and the life of Jesus to my sisters and me. We often sat together on the living room sofa after supper, listening to Dad read to us before bedtime. He read from our Bible storybooks with their colorful illustrations and then retold the stories in his own words. "How does Jesus love me like a good shepherd?" I asked, not knowing what a shepherd was. "Jesus was like Uncle Les on the farm, caring for his baby lambs. Do you remember the sheep and baby lambs we saw on the farm this summer?" Dad asked. We lived in the country and often visited Aunt Mary and Uncle Les on their farm, so Dad's story helped me understand the meaning of Jesus as a good shepherd. "A good shepherd watches out for all his sheep," said Dad, explaining the meaning of the Bible story in the gospel of John. "If even one lamb is lost, he'll find that lost sheep and keep it safe from harm. A good shepherd will do anything to take care of his sheep. That's how Jesus is–he watches over us and keeps us safe."

Every Sunday, cardboard fans with wooden handles were placed in all the church pews, each depicting a picture from Jesus' life. During sweltering summer church services, we relied on those fans for faint relief, with the pictures leaving a lasting impression. They showed scenes of lambs and little children on Jesus' lap, his crucifixion on a cross, and his resurrection with a shining halo around his head. During services, hymns echoed my dad's stories, such as "What a Friend We Have in Jesus" and "The Old Rugged Cross." The story of Jesus returning to life after three days was fascinating. It was a miracle, and like most young children, I found it magical, awe-inspiring, and a totally believable story.

After I learned the Bible stories and could repeat them, I "pronounced my faith" to the whole church congregation when I was seven years old, with about 150 people sitting in the pews watching. Dressed in my best Sunday dress, black patent leather Mary Jane shoes, and white frilly socks, I walked to the front of the church during the final hymn. I told my dad, who presided over the service, that I believed the stories and wanted to be a Christian and join the church. I wasn't nervous about going in front of the congregation because I recognized most of these people, one of the benefits of being a preacher's kid. The following Sunday, I was baptized before all the church members to symbolize and confirm my childhood Christian conversion.

I had seen baptisms many times, but when my day arrived, I felt my anxiety rise. The baptism occurred in a large pool of water behind the altar and in front of a life-sized, painted mural of John baptizing Jesus. The pool was like a big rectangular stone bathtub with steps descending into the water that came up to my father's waist. I stood at the top of the stairs and felt scared as I looked down the steps, afraid I would slip and fall. Dad had on a white robe over his clothes, like the choir members, and I wore a white robe, too. He smiled reassuringly and stood barefoot in the pool of water with outstretched hands, waiting for me to join him. I felt nervous as I stepped into the pool, also barefoot, feeling the lukewarm water move up my legs. Dad reached out and took my hands as I gingerly walked down each step. With the water all around us, he held me in his strong arms, carefully covered my nose and mouth with one hand, and then immersed me fully under the water. As everyone watched the immersion, he spoke loudly and warmly, "I baptize you, Susanne, in the name of the Father, and of the Son, and of the Holy Ghost." Taking a quick breath, I emerged from the water and walked up the pool steps, dripping. I felt relieved and happy. From that day forward, I was dedicated to my faith and aimed to please my parents and God.

At the end of my second-grade year, we moved to Red Springs in the "down-East" area of the state, fewer than 100 miles from the beach. Southern Baptist churches select their own ministers rather than following the direction of a denominational hierarchy. After five years in Olive Chapel, Dad received a call to accept a new position as minister of the town's First Baptist Church. This town of 2,500 people was in Robeson County, noted for having an evenly divided triracial population of white, Black, and Indigenous people, the Lumbee tribe. In those days, the Lumbee people were not recognized as an Indigenous Nation, and they seemed to be at the bottom of the racial hierarchy. In 1958, when I was 11 years old, the Ku Klux Klan attacked them in an armed raid on their community. The raid made big news both nationally and in the state,[2] and Dad led a group of people from our church to the neighboring town of Pembroke to help the Lumbee people with home repairs and food. This raid marked the first time I learned about the KKK and how violence can be linked to racism, and I was worried Dad would also be hurt by helping those who had been injured.

In those years of total segregation in Southern states, the small town of Red Springs had three public schools. Each included grades 1 through 12 and matched the names on the three public water fountains on Main Street, labeled "White," "Negro," and "Indian." I rarely saw people who were not white, except on Saturdays when folks came to town to shop. However, Mom hired a Black woman who ironed our clothes several times a month. She lived with her family across the railroad tracks at the end of the street where we lived, and I occasionally played with her daughter when Mom took me to visit.

In hindsight, Red Springs reminds me of descriptions of the racist Alabama town in *To Kill a Mockingbird*,[3] including Boo Radley's scary house down the street from our church parsonage. The old house with once-white peeling paint and overgrown weeds frightened me. I would run past it on my way to the white school on Main Street.

The First Baptist Church was also located on Main Street. I attended church twice a day on Sundays, attended prayer meetings and church suppers on Wednesday nights, and joined weekly meetings of the Girls' Auxiliary (GAs), the Baptist version of the Girl Scouts. In GAs, I learned more Bible stories and memorized verses for badges and a cardboard crown. When I attended an outdoor Vacation Bible School one summer, I began to experience my first questions, leading to doubts about the truthfulness of my Christian beliefs. Under the shade of giant live oak trees, my friends and I sat around picnic tables on the church front lawn, listening to stories about missionaries in other countries. We colored pictures and sang the children's song:

Jesus loves the little children,
all the children of the world,
Red and Yellow, Black and White,
They are precious in his sight
Jesus loves the children of the world.

In the heat of that afternoon, I realized that all the world's children might not know Jesus as I did. I was not doubting the existence of God at this point, but I questioned how God could send children in other countries to hell if they had never even heard of Jesus.

Despite my questions, I continued to feel confident that God loved me. This love was affirmed when our family went to Caswell with other church members on week-long summer trips. Fort Caswell had been built on the coast of North Carolina in 1836 to guard the port of nearby Wilmington, and the military base was bought by the State Baptist Assembly in 1949 to welcome church groups for summer retreats. I loved going there with my family and friends, swimming in the ocean, and watching artists lead "chalk talks" outside the old military barracks in the afternoons. Artists would draw with large pieces of chalk on flip charts while illustrating the Bible stories they told. Since I liked to draw, I was amazed as I watched the pictures emerge on the oversized white newsprint propped on the artist's easel.

I hated picking the painful sand spurs out of my feet when I ran barefoot across the large lawn at Fort Caswell, but I liked climbing up the tall iron ladders to the top of the flat roof of the old fort that overlooked the Atlantic Ocean. The fort was tall enough for me to see 360 degrees in all directions. I would sit on the roof, cross-legged with dozens of people for the Vesper services every night at sunset. Although I was a young child, these sunset Vespers were the most meaningful part of the week for me, even more than the chalk talks. I was in awe as I looked east out over the ocean waves and then turned to watch the sky turn red and gold as the sun slipped beneath the western horizon. The Vespers' speaker assured us, "God loves you and knows you, just as he counts and knows each grain of sand on this ocean floor." Watching that sunset and the ocean waves, while hearing the speaker's promise, created a mystical experience etched in my pre-adolescent mind as I tried to make sense of the vastness of God's love.

I was also trying to make sense of my place in the world and my privilege. My Dad was well-respected in Baptist religious circles in our state, and adults sometimes told me, "You are so lucky to be Willis Bennett's daughter." One warm summer afternoon when I was ten years old, I was lying alone on my back on the lawn behind our church, looking up into a cloudless sky. When I turned over to examine the grass, I saw countless four-leaf clovers everywhere around me. I had never seen so many at once, and I couldn't help but wonder: "Am I lucky or what?" Even today, I still wonder about what I saw that day. "Am I lucky? Or do I see things others don't see? Was it just random luck that I happened to be there that summer day, or am I truly lucky to be who I am?" I also wonder, "What does it mean when people say I am so lucky to be Willis Bennett's daughter?" I've contemplated these questions throughout my life, trying to discern what to do with the blessing of being born to parents who showed me their love and the other privileges I enjoyed.

Upon reflection, I realize my early childhood faith exemplifies a faith of "simplicity," the first of McLaren's four stages of faith development.[4] McLaren identifies this initial stage of faith as a period of "simplicity," which occurs approximately in the first twelve years of a child's life. Simplicity revolves around dependence on authority figures, such as parents, grandparents, teachers, and religious leaders. In this stage, children focus on seeing the world in a dualistic manner, sorting the world into twos, such as good or bad, right or wrong. McLaren says the simplicity stage of faith is founded on "simple trust; simple obedience; simple, unquestioning loyalty."[5]

As a child, I trusted that my authority figures had all the correct answers. I **unquestionably accepted what I thought my parents believed.** I focused on right and wrong and wanted to please my parents and God. Like most young children, I saw the world in twos: good or bad, happy or sad, glad or mad, in or out, up or down. In other words, the simplicity of my faith saw the world in a dualistic manner.

McLaren proposes that we progress from one phase of faith to the next by experiencing doubt, which leads to growth through questioning our current life assumptions. The process of questioning and experiencing doubt began in earnest when I was 12, and my family moved from North Carolina to Kentucky. My father accepted a position as Professor of Church and Community at The Southern

Baptist Theological Seminary in Louisville. In July 1959, my family and I took the two-day, 600-mile journey from Red Springs to Louisville, with our belongings following in a separate moving van. My sisters and I were in the backseat, playing games of counting sheep and "I spy" to pass the time as we drove through the countryside heading Northwest. These were the days when many highways were still two-lane roads, not the broad Interstates that now pave the journey from one state to the next.

Somewhere along the two-lane road, a gigantic tractor-trailer came barreling toward us head-on while it was trying to pass a car. My sisters and I screamed and closed our eyes; I was sure the truck was going to crash into us. Dad quickly swerved off the highway onto the shoulder, the car resting at the edge of a deep ditch. We were all stunned and in shock as we sat in dead silence. Dad looked shaken, and Mom patted his shoulder and tried to comfort him as he resumed driving. My sisters and I cried softly in the backseat, too frightened to speak. That traumatic event stuck in my mind for the remainder of the trip as we headed to our new home. I believed we came close to being killed, and I saw our near collision as a sign of what might lie ahead.

I had been afraid of moving and was already missing my girlfriends. I was still determining how I would fit into my new school, Waggener High, which included grades 7 through 12 and had a larger student population than our whole town of Red Springs. Trying to prepare me, Mom and Dad told me Waggener was racially integrated, which both excited and frightened me. However, our new home was located on the east side of Louisville, in St. Matthews, which was primarily white. In the days before busing-enforced integration, it turned out that my school had very few People of Color. I didn't know what to expect at Waggener, but I sensed my life would change. I was beginning to have questions that would push me out of the cocoon of the innocent views of my childhood. "What will my new life be like? Will I ever make good friends again? Why did we have to move anyway?" The near-death experience on the highway en route to our new home felt ominous.

I would soon turn 13, and the world would turn upside down as the decade of the 1960s unfolded during my adolescence. I didn't know the significance of the forthcoming cultural changes, but I knew my life was moving differently. Looking back, my transitions from childhood into adolescence and young adulthood were profound. The challenges I experienced during these years confirm the words of McLaren, who says: "There is faith after doubt, and life after doubt, and life with doubt.... wait until you see where doubt can lead you and what doubt can teach you."[6]

On Children

By Khalil Gibran

Your children are not your children.
They are the sons and daughters of Life's longing for
itself.
They come through you but not from you,
And though they are with you yet they belong not to
you.

You may give them your love but not your thoughts,
For they have their own thoughts.
You may house their bodies but not their souls,
For their souls dwell in the house of tomorrow, which
you cannot visit,
not even in your dreams.
You may strive to be like them, but seek not to make
them like you.
For life goes not backward nor tarries with yesterday.

—Gibran, K. (1923). On Children. *The Prophet.*
New York: Knoph Publisher, pp. 17-18.

Two

High School Questions

When you get your "Who am I?" question right,

all the "What should I do?" questions

tend to take care of themselves.

—*Richard Rohr*[1]

When we moved to Louisville, Kentucky, the large new church we joined, Highland Baptist, had an active youth group led by one of the graduate students at Southern Seminary, where my father was teaching. Our youth director seemed eager to teach us what he was learning in his classes, though some of what he imparted surprised me.

Under our leader's guidance, I learned new ways of interpreting the Bible, and he told us that some stories were inaccurately translated into English and were not literally true. He said Mary was not a virgin, as we understood the word in contemporary English, because the word in Hebrew actually meant "young girl or young woman." I felt liberated hearing this perspective because it answered my question: "How could Jesus be born to a virgin?" As I moved into puberty and learned more about sexuality, the "Virgin Mary" story no longer made sense. The instruction and discussions in my youth group expanded my understanding of what I had been taught when I was younger. Learning new interpretations of the Bible from a reputable teacher in my church allowed me to break away from my childhood literalism. I began to question and reconsider the religious views of my younger years.

I was also influenced by the broader cultural upheaval at the time, particularly the beginning of the Civil Rights Movement. As a family, we watched and discussed the news every night on our black and white TV set inside its brown wooden cabinet, and we regularly read *The Louisville Courier-Journal* newspaper and *Look, Life, Time,* and *Newsweek* magazines. My sheltered world was starting to crack as new knowledge and the culture challenged my childhood beliefs. I was aware and curious about the "Freedom Riders," white and Black college students riding on buses to go South to Mississippi to protest and help people register to vote; four Black children killed by a bomb in a Birmingham, Alabama, Baptist Church; and Black people sitting at lunch counters in Greensboro, N.C., and in the front seats of buses in Montgomery, AL. I knew about Martin Luther King, Jr. and what he was preaching, and I was aware of my parents' interest and convictions about these issues. Dr. King came to the Seminary in 1961, and Dad helped sponsor his visit and personally met with him.

Soon after Dr. King's visit, Dad received permission to obtain his Master of Social Work (MSW) degree at the University of Louisville with the goal of establishing a joint Social Work-Divinity program at the seminary, the first dual degree of its kind in the country. He had begun his academic career as the seminary's "Church and Community" professor based on the Christian belief that we are called to be involved and active in the life of the community around us. He had spent his ministry in North Carolina with that mission in mind, demonstrated by his involvement with the farmers in Olive Chapel and his assistance with the Lumbee tribe in Red Springs. Although he already had a Masters in Divinity and a PhD in Theology, Dad obtained his additional MSW, paid for by the seminary, to better educate prospective ministers about engaging with the world.

In addition to my awareness and interest in the Civil Rights Movement, I developed a strong interest in national politics. As a young teen, I watched the Democratic National Convention in 1960 and, a few months later, saw John F. Kennedy be sworn in as the first Catholic President of the United States. I was infatuated by his youth, handsome looks, intelligence, charisma, and New England background. My parents also expressed support for President Kennedy. Although some Protestants worried the Pope would control President Kennedy because he was Catholic, Dad expressed confidence there would be a separation of church and state as defined in the U.S. Constitution.

I was a high school junior in my advanced level art class when I heard the news announced over the school's loudspeaker on Friday afternoon, November 22, 1963. President Kennedy had been shot. We stopped our class and huddled around a radio to hear further updates. Waggener's football team was scheduled to play a major game that Friday night, and a pep rally was planned for that afternoon. Eventually, students throughout the whole school quietly moved into the hallways and stood, watching the uniformed cheerleaders and football players walk down the halls between us, moving in reverent silence toward the gymnasium for the pep rally that didn't occur. Students slowly gathered in the gym, where we learned more details. President Kennedy was dead. I was devastated and began to weep with many in the large room full of students. We were in shock. School was dismissed early, and the football game was postponed.

Over that grey and cold November weekend, my family and I watched around-the-clock news coverage on TV, repeatedly playing the motorcade assassination footage, then the solemn funeral and the burial at Arlington Cemetery on November 25th, where the eternal flame was lit in Kennedy's honor. President Kennedy's death seemed to launch a massive national upheaval in the years ahead, marked by the Vietnam War, the growing violence of the Civil Rights Movement, the assassination of Malcolm X in 1965, and then in 1968, the assassinations of both Robert Kennedy and Martin Luther King, Jr. President Kennedy remained a powerful symbol of hope for me and inspired my lifelong interest in national politics. His death also heightened my awareness of how the world can change dramatically in one moment in time.

During my high school years, Dad and I often engaged in meaningful conversations about politics, civil rights, poverty, and social justice. He told me about his social work field placements, and Mom shared about her work as a typing teacher in a large all-Black school in downtown Louisville. "How is it fair that we're middle class, and there are so many people in this city who are poor?" I asked them. "And why are we considered poor compared to other people at my school?" I was trying to understand class differences and why we were so relatively privileged, so lucky, compared to the kids in Mom's school, yet I felt poor at my own school.

I went to one of the wealthiest public high schools in the Louisville area at that time, but money was tight in our family. Despite my father's prominence in our religious circles, I felt different from my upper-middle-class friends who belonged to private swim clubs that we couldn't afford. I comforted myself with the many Bible verses I knew by heart. As a teen, I recalled Jesus' words: "It is easier for a camel to go through a needle's eye than for a rich man to enter into the kingdom of God" (Mathew 19:24, RSV). Still, I felt confused and guilty about feeling envious of my more economically privileged Waggener friends.

My adolescent questions about faith joined my questions about social class and civil rights, and all these questions intensified in my junior and senior years at Waggener. Influenced by my assigned readings, I began to piece together my new understandings. I came to disbelieve the existence of hell after reading Dante's *Inferno*.[2] I became aware of religions worldwide by reading Huston Smith's *The Religions of Man*,[3] and I started to doubt Christianity was the best religion or the one for me. I learned about Judaism, the Holocaust, and the horrors perpetrated by the Nazis when I read Victor Frankl's *Man's Search for Meaning*.[4] Exposure to this knowledge and historical perspective expanded my vision, and I began to ponder the meaning and purpose of my own life and to ask myself, "Who am I?"

In addition to my academic coursework, I was influenced by my engagement in the community. Between my junior and senior years in high school, I had my first summer job as a social work intern at a large Baptist church in downtown Louisville. My dad found this job for me through his connection with the new social work school established at the seminary. Admittedly, I needed more clarity about my responsibilities and had little supervision for this work. However, I developed an activity program for elementary-age children and responded to the requests for help from people in the neighborhood. One hot summer day, a Black single mother with seven children called the church requesting money for food for her family. After getting funds from the church, I drove to the grocery store and bought her a hundred dollars' worth of groceries, which was a lot of food in those days. I had never bought groceries by myself, and I tried to think about what my mom bought for our family meals. Among other staples, I purchased this family a baked ham, sweet potatoes, and canned green beans because I was concerned fresh foods might not last.

When I took the groceries to this woman's small apartment, I was stunned by the level of poverty I saw. A tattered sofa, table, and a few old chairs were in the room, and the younger children were all around their mother, looking scared and staring hesitantly at me. I suddenly realized I didn't have a clue what I was doing. The woman and I had no idea what to say to each other. I awkwardly set down the grocery bags and left. Afterward, I sensed I should have just given this woman the money to buy her food. I worried she felt humiliated or angry about having a white teenage girl bring her groceries. That evening, I had a long conversation with my dad about poverty and racism, as well as the different views of Martin Luther King Jr. and Malcolm X. Dad was aligned with the nonviolent stance of Dr. King, but I sympathized with the views of Malcolm X. He seemed to me to capture the anger people would feel if they lived in poverty like the woman I met that day.

My community involvement and academic coursework made me feel I wanted to serve others who were less privileged than me. I began to feel I should be an activist like the college students going to Mississippi or join the newly created Peace Corps to work with underserved people in other countries. I had an older cousin who had just joined the Peace Corps after college, so I was captivated by it. When I was 10, I wanted to be a missionary to Africa, like the missionaries I met in my church. Although by age 17 I had let go of that dream, I still strongly desired to serve people who were suffering or in need of help, though I needed clarification on what that meant. I just knew I was deeply moved by the poverty in downtown Louisville, distressed by the horrors of concentration camps, and intrigued by other world religions. Buddhism, with its emphasis on human suffering, especially sparked my interest. My parents were role models for me regarding their vocations serving others, so I believed they would understand if I talked with them about my developing vocational interests.

After reading the chapter on Buddhism in *The Religions of Man* in my senior Humanities class, I decided to reach out to my parents to discuss these ideas further. Mom and Dad had always supported my personal and intellectual growth and encouraged my questions about social issues or vocational interests. "Dad," I said one night at the dinner table. "I just learned about Buddhism in my class at school. What do you know about it? I never realized it was such a big world religion." There was a pause, and then I added, "I think I want to become a Zen Buddhist." I no longer recall his response at the dinner table, but I'll never forget what happened after dinner.

I went upstairs to my room to do my homework, and about a half hour later, he stormed into my bedroom. He threw a book onto my bed where I was sitting. Gowans' 1930 book, titled *Why I Believe*,[5] is still in my possession. While I cried, he yelled angrily, "I've spent my whole life teaching you about Christianity. How can you dare question it?" This wasn't a two-way discussion. He expressed his disappointment in me and insisted that I read his book (which I never did). He looked as if he were about to cry. I was shocked, too afraid and upset to defend myself or even respond. In my head, I privately yelled, "You can't tell me what to think!" After that day, I became cautious about sharing my new beliefs with my father, especially my doubts about Christianity. While both my parents were forthcoming about their views and encouraged me to be similarly honest, I became selective about what I shared as I matured. I trusted they would always love me, but I tried to avoid arguments and their disappointment about my changing perspectives. For several years, I harbored resentment towards my father for not welcoming my evolving religious views.

My interest in Buddhism as a 17-year-old and the questioning of my Christian beliefs illustrate McLaren's second stage of faith development, which he terms "complexity." This stage often begins in adolescence as young people question the stories they were taught at a younger age. Adolescents frequently question and look for new ways to interpret their childhood beliefs, especially when they once believed in literal Biblical interpretations. They individuate from their childhood authority figures and turn their attention to the development of new friendships. Questioning and individuating are common and healthy traits for the psychosocial development of adolescents and will naturally also impact a young person's faith development.

As a child, I had learned that Christianity was the one and only path to God, but I was looking for new ways to interpret what I had been taught. My interest in other world religions opened the door for me toward new ways of thinking. The stage of complexity is a period of expanding interest beyond childhood authority figures, and I became firmly interested in that process during my high school years.

As part of expanding beyond parental authority, socializing with friends takes primary importance, and developing romantic friendships is a typical part of socializing during adolescence. Like most teens, my sexual interests blossomed during those years. In addition to broadening my perspectives on politics, civil rights, and faith, I began exploring my sexuality and questioning family rules about how "good girls" should behave.

As I pushed my boundaries, my parents and I had more frequent arguments. We often argued about my independence related to my social life and breaking their rules. Mom was critical about how I spent my allowance. She would tearfully exclaim: "How can you take your father's hard-earned money and spend it on cigarettes?" Dad would become upset and disapproving when I invited boys to visit our house after school when no adults were home. I exploded at him in anger one day about all my restrictions, actually yelling with out-of-control adolescent rage: "I hate you!" Amazingly, he remained calm, unfazed, and said, "I know you hate me right now, but I still love you." Though I was egging for a fight, his response melted my anger. Despite tense parental attempts to set age-appropriate boundaries, I generally experienced our family as lively and fun. I also never doubted Mom and Dad loved me. They maintained a balance between managing my growing independence while remaining available and supportive when I needed them.

⸙

When I was in eighth grade, my parents started letting me go to boy-girl group parties with classmates, and there were several boys I especially noticed and liked in this group of friends. I discovered the pleasure and excitement of making out with boys. By the beginning of ninth grade, my favorite boyfriend was Ted, and within a few months, Ted gave me his ring, the token of the time. We began "going steady," meaning we only dated each other.

Ted was a good-looking guy who fit my handsome dreamboat image with the looks of my 1960s teen idols, and he and I went steady our freshman through junior years in high school. For over two years, we talked on the phone every night after school and went to parties on the weekends, where we mastered the art of the twist to Motown music. We spent a lot of time exploring our sexual relationship, making out, and fumbling around with each other. I used to write "Mrs. Ted Quincy" on all my school notebooks, imagining my future married life with him. Although my faith development was in a stage of complexity during my adolescence, my initial sexual development fit better with a stage of simplicity. I was following the authority of the teachings of my church about what was right versus wrong in terms of sexual expression. Based on how I interpreted my religious messages, I should not express my sexual feelings for Ted beyond allowing him to go to "second base."

As I approached my senior year in high school and became more thoughtful about my future and the meaning of my life, I began to lose interest in Ted. He insisted we "go all the way," but I was not a willing partner. As a preteen, I had signed an abstinence pledge in church that I would remain a virgin until I married, and I was determined to keep that pledge. In addition, birth control was not readily available for teenagers at that time. A girl in one of my classes at school had disappeared for a year and then returned. The rumor was that she had gone out of town to have a baby that she released for adoption. Her experience made me afraid of getting pregnant out of wedlock. I broke up with Ted rather than have sex out of marriage.

Nevertheless, I still enjoyed romantic play, and during my senior year in high school, I had two other boyfriends who never pushed me for sex, as Ted had done. Although I took real pleasure in dating and exploring my sexual relationships with boys, I had clear views about what was right and wrong in terms of expressing myself sexually. My sexual views had not moved into a stage of complexity, like my faith.

Abstinence Pledge Example

"True Love Waits"

"Believing that true love waits,
I make a commitment
to God, myself, my family, my friends,
my future mate, and my future children
to be sexually abstinent
from this day until the day
I enter a Biblical marriage relationship."

—Southern Baptist Convention (1991). *True Love Waits*.
Retrieved from Encyclopedia.com.

.

Three

College Complexity

Doubt is the mother of conviction...

It is doubt that is the beginning of real faith.

—*Joan Chittister & Rowan Williams*[1]

After graduating from high school in 1965, I left Kentucky and returned to North Carolina for college, attending Wake Forest, which became a university in 1967. I had heard of this school my whole life because my father had graduated from the college when it was initially located in the small town of Wake Forest, near Raleigh. Established in 1834, "Old Wake Forest" moved 100 miles to Winston-Salem in 1956 after the Z. Smith Reynolds Foundation donated the land from the large estate of the tobacco magnate, R.J. Reynolds. Wake Forest was my top choice among the Southern Baptist colleges I considered.

The campus, with its all-brick Georgian architecture and magnolia trees, still had a new look when I began as a freshman in September 1965. At one end of the quad was Wake Chapel, a beautiful building with a tall steeple symbolic of the university's religious affiliation with the Southern Baptists. Students attended required weekly chapel, campus-wide meetings, and conferences in Wake Chapel, which also housed the religion department. At the other end of the long, rectangular quad was Reynolda Hall, the stately administrative building, with the offices of the President, Deans, and registrar. All dining facilities and additional rooms for student gatherings were located there.

"Old Wake Forest" was initially an all-male college, and even though women were admitted in 1942, there were still more men than women when I began 23 years later. The men's dorms lined the quad between the administrative building and chapel, with tall maple trees surrounding an open grass lawn at the quad's center. The library, academic buildings, and women's dorms were outside the quad. When my friends and I had to walk from our dorm to the other end of campus for classes in the chapel, we had to walk by fraternity guys sitting on the low walls in front of their dorms, making catcalls as we passed.

I immediately fell in love with Wake Forest and soon began making friends in my freshman dorm. The junior dorm advisor and I became good buddies toward the end of my freshman year, and she encouraged me to try out for the college newspaper as a writer. She was a reporter for *The Old Gold & Black* and became editor of the paper the following year. Her ulterior motive in having me join the paper staff may have been to meet her friend, Robert, a sophomore and an *Old Gold* reporter. I did begin writing for the paper, but the highlight of my college journalism career was meeting Robert.

When I returned to campus for my sophomore year, Robert and I began spending many hours together in *The Old Gold & Black* office on "pub row," the administration building floor where the paper, yearbook, and school radio station were located. We soon began dating. I was attracted to Robert's personality and appearance—a slender six foot two inches with brunette hair, dark brown eyes, and

studious-looking horn-rimmed glasses. I adored his
Southern drawl, his humor and quick wit, and,
occasionally, his sarcasm. He was a talented writer and
editor and became a mentor for me when I was a cub
reporter.

I knew I was attracted to Robert one autumn day
when we took a long walk in the beautiful Reynolda
Gardens, which included many acres of informal and
formal gardens adjacent to the main campus. We sat on a
large tree limb, jutting out over a burbling spring in the
secluded wooded area of the informal gardens and talked
for hours. We shared detailed, in-depth stories about our
families and upbringing, and I learned what we had in
common along with how we were raised in very different
families. He grew up in a troubled family with his mother,
six siblings, and an alcoholic father, and he was determined
to be different from his father.

I also wanted to be different from my father, as I felt
misunderstood by him at the time, specifically after my
failed efforts to discuss my changing religious views with
him. I craved recognition for my ideas and felt that Robert
understood and valued me. I was drawn to him partly
because of our shared backgrounds, growing up in North
Carolina, being active in the Baptist church, and being
students in a large urban public high school. His humor
reminded me of my mom, and his serious approach to the
news and commitment to civil rights reminded me of my
dad. But what most attracted me was our mutual empathy

for each other. In hindsight, I also felt drawn to caring for him after hearing about his family.

꧁꧂

In addition to developing my romantic relationship with Robert during college, I focused on creating academic and spiritual ideas separate from my parents. My questions about my faith multiplied exponentially, beginning in my freshman year. In those years, Wake Forest still required all students to take introductory courses in the Old and New Testaments. In my freshman year Old Testament course, my professor taught us that many stories in the Hebrew scriptures consist of truths more profound than facts; we should not take these words literally but understand their context instead. I felt apprehensive about what I was learning. As a young child, I thought faith meant believing in the Bible's truthfulness without question. As I began to learn how to apply Biblical criticism and incorporate the insights of scholars and theologians, questions about the religious teachings of my childhood intensified. In addition, I stopped going to church most Sundays, a complete change from my childhood. There was an active Baptist church on campus, with services held in Wake Chapel, but I rarely attended.

My most meaningful freshman-year academic experience was writing a Biblical criticism of the legend in Genesis 22 about God asking Abraham to sacrifice his son Isaac as a burnt offering. Initially, I was confused and drawn to this story because I wondered if my father would sacrifice or kill me if God told him to do so. The story and God's command didn't make sense to me. In my search for clarification, I read Biblical commentators who went deeper into the history and meaning of the legend. I discovered that the Danish theologian and existential philosopher Soren Kierkegaard had written a treatise about the story of Abraham and Isaac. Sitting in the crowded, dark confines of the large library's lower basement stacks, I spent hours reading and trying to understand Kierkegaard's complicated famous 1843 treatise, *Fear and Trembling*.[2]

Eventually, I realized that Kierkegaard proposed that the story of Abraham and Isaac describes a "paradox of faith." That is, faith means trusting in God and believing in God's goodness, even when God's words seem irrational, unethical, and make no sense. The paradox is holding onto the contradictory belief that God is good, though God may ask us to suspend what ordinarily seems to be ethical. When God commands Abraham to kill his only son, Kierkegaard says Abraham took a "leap of faith" by obeying God without question and suspending what was ethical, reasonable, and rational. When Abraham proceeded to follow God's command, placing Issac on top of the altar of wood and taking out a knife to slay his son, God told Abraham: "For now I know that you fear God, seeing you have not withheld your son, your only son, from me" (Gn. 22:12 RSV). Then, God commanded Abraham to substitute a nearby ram as the burnt offering instead of Isaac.

I had an epiphany while writing this scholarly paper. It was the first time I realized I could interpret the Bible based on my understanding of Biblical criticism, theology, and Biblical interpretation. I no longer needed to follow what my father or church teachers taught me to believe when I was younger. I thought they wanted me to accept *their* words and interpretations without questions. When I incorporated Kierkegaard's ideas into my critique of the Genesis legend, I experienced a clarity I had not previously known. I became clear that I trusted God and felt God's love despite my uncertainties about God's existence and power. Like Abraham, my faith was not a rational belief based on what made sense or based on what my parents had taught me to believe. I also became clear about my independent capacity to understand complicated ideas, which helped to increase my academic self-confidence.

By my junior year, I declared my major in religion and embraced Paul Tillich's theology in his 1957 book, *The Dynamics of Faith*.[3] In a paper on faith and doubt, I applied Tillich's ideas to Psalm 22, which begins: "My God, my God, why have you forsaken me?" I still have that paper, written nearly 60 years ago, and I feel reassured when I read it today. As a paraphrase of Tillich and, perhaps, a precursor to McLaren, I concluded:

> *Doubt is an inevitable element of faith, not a negation of faith. Although it is not a permanent element within the act of faith, doubt is a part of every religious life, which fluctuates from confident certainty to despairing*

*uncertainty...after each new leap of faith, doubt and
uncertainties may appear anew.*

During this realization about faith, I continued to
question the existence of God as I approached college
graduation. Nietzsche's famous statement, "God is dead,"[4]
inspired the "God is Dead" movement in the 1960s. When I
was in college, numerous theologians and philosophers
tried to make sense of the growing secularism in 20th-
century culture, and some proposed that the Christian God
of their era was no longer relevant due to secularism. I read
Gabriel Vahanian's 1961 book, *The Death of God*,[5] exploring
God's relevancy and lamenting the loss of the sacred in
modern culture. Tillich also explored the ideas of Nietzsche
in his 1957 book, *The Courage to Be*. He said: "The courage to
be is rooted in the God who appears when God disappears
in the anxiety of doubt."[6] These ideas influenced me and
prompted me to call myself a "Christian agnostic," which I
defined as questioning God's existence while accepting the
historical Jesus as a world-changing prophet.

My faith stage of complexity began in high school.
During college, I became firmly grounded in my
independent thinking, making sense of my world based on
the new theological ideas I was exploring. I was no longer a
dependent child, so I focused on self-reliance and finding a
way to live my own life. In college, my intellectual and

critical views supported my individuation from my family's beliefs. Majoring in religion looked on the surface like I was identifying with my father because he was a minister and seminary professor. Instead, my academic study of religion enabled me to individuate from him and find my own voice and explanations.

Through this life-shaping and complex process of differentiating from my parents and deconstructing my faith, I felt the support and empathy of my religion professors. Some of them knew my father and my religious upbringing, and they realized the significant transition I was undergoing. My primary mentor was my Old Testament professor, Dr. Phyllis Trible, who later became a nationally renowned Biblical scholar. In one of my papers, she once wrote a quote from Zen Buddhist Hsin-hsin Mind: "If you want to get to the plain truth, be not concerned with right and wrong. The conflict between right and wrong is the sickness of the mind." This way of thinking was reassuring and sustaining, and it moved me toward seeing the world through a more holistic lens.

I'm not sure my father ever knew how much I moved away from the form of Christianity that was central to his life. I developed some significant differences with him regarding Christian theology, such as doubting his unquestioning belief in the bodily resurrection of Jesus. However, I knew he trusted the overall legitimacy of what I was learning, even if it was far from my religious education as a young child. Dad's college roommate was a Wake Forest religion department professor, and our two families were friends. I always felt that long-standing connection reassured my Dad about the validity of my academic studies of religion. Despite our differences regarding theology, I modeled my life after my father in terms of his courage to take strong stands based on his convictions, especially regarding social justice issues. I admired him, and I felt his support. By the time I finished college, I had let go of the hurt I felt toward him in high school, when I believed he misunderstood me. However, I still had a sense my religious convictions would continue to move away from his as I moved further into adulthood.

My faith development fits with the complexity stage of faith through deconstructing my childhood religious views. However, my simple and innocent relationship with Robert was not complex. We continued to date throughout college, and our relationship was safe and traditional. By his senior year—my junior year—Robert was the editor of the *Old Gold & Black*, and I was the feature editor and cartoonist. We spent most of our time on pub row in the newspaper office, meeting the deadline of a weekly paper. We also had fun regularly going off campus to eat and to the movies, and once, we drove a hundred miles to Raleigh to see Diana Ross and the Supremes in the nose-bleed seats at the Coliseum. Yet, honestly, our relationship was rather staid and not too passionate. I never worried he was going to insist that we have sex. I was still living in a stage of innocent simplicity and following my childhood expectations about how a courtship should be before marriage.

51

At the end of my junior year, Robert and I were walking in the formal English garden in Reynolda Gardens and stopped to stand under pink tulip magnolias in their early spring bloom. In his romantic way, he put his arms around me and then asked me to marry him as he pulled a velvet box out of his pocket. I immediately said, "Yes!" He slipped a beautiful, small diamond on my left ring finger. I felt confident that he was the right man for me. I loved him deeply and didn't want to wait until after I graduated to get married. I was saving myself for him, and I didn't want to put off the wedding for another year.

We made plans to marry at the end of August, about four months after we became engaged. After graduating, Robert stayed in North Carolina to work as a reporter for a local newspaper near the beach. His professional goal was to be a journalist, and this summer job set him on his way. I spent that summer at home in Louisville planning our wedding. We planned a formal evening wedding at my church, with a non-alcoholic reception in the fellowship hall following the service since Baptists didn't drink. Robert and I planned to have five attendants each, including our friends and four siblings. My mom helped me with the invitations, flowers, photography, and wedding cake. A family friend who was a seamstress made my traditional long white satin and lace wedding gown with a train and floor-length chiffon veil. She had also made my yellow prom dress in high school. Reflecting on how much goes into planning large weddings today, I am amazed mine came together so quickly and without much trouble, with the loving support of my family and our community.

Benediction

By Brian McLaren

Blessed are the curious,

for their curiosity honors reality

Blessed are the uncertain and those with second thoughts,

for their minds are still open.

Blessed are the wonderers,

for they shall find what is wonderful.

Blessed are those who question their answers,

for their horizons will expand forever.

Blessed are the doubters,

for they shall see through fake gods.

Blessed are the lovers,

for they shall see God everywhere.

—Brian McLaren (2021). *Faith after doubt*.
New York: St. Martin's Publishing Group, pp. 218-219.

Part Two

_____

Young Adulthood

Four

Marriage and Divorce

Darkness deserves gratitude.

It is the alleluia point at which we learn to understand

that all growth does not take place in the sunlight.

—*Joan Chittister*[1]

I married Robert at Highland Baptist Church in Louisville, the church of my adolescence. In August 1968, my father walked me down the aisle and then officiated my Saturday night candlelight wedding ceremony. The large church sanctuary was packed, primarily with our relatives and friends of my parents; only a few close friends from college attended. At age 21, I followed the expectations for young women of my era who had grown up in the South. We married young, before the Women's Movement influenced our world and before Stonewall and the Gay Liberation Movement came on the scene.

Robert and I had a brief honeymoon on our way from Kentucky back to North Carolina, where he planned to begin work as a local newspaper reporter in Winston-Salem, and I planned to finish my final year of college. We took a meandering drive through the Appalachian Mountains and stayed a few days in the vacation resort town of Gatlinburg, Tennessee, "the gateway to the Smokies." The ground-level room of our small inn was the perfect, quiet honeymoon getaway, surrounded by tall evergreens and sliding glass doors that opened to a soothing mountain brook. Yet, as we cuddled in bed, Robert seemed preoccupied, and we spent most of our time watching the protests at the 1968 Democratic National

Convention. Four days after our wedding, we tuned in to watch the police and anti-Vietnam War protestors rioting in Chicago, chanting, "The whole world is watching!" We watched with the world and continued watching through most of our honeymoon. In hindsight, our preoccupation with external political events likely distracted us from pursuing our intimate relationship, which proved an inauspicious beginning to our marriage.

Over the next two years, I graduated from college and then taught third graders in a nearby rural school, the next county over. Robert worked a year as a reporter and then transitioned to being editor of Wake Forest's alumni magazine and assistant to the University President. After these first years of married life, we were excited when he received an offer to be a reporter for *The Baltimore Sun*. Our move to Baltimore felt to me like our first significant adult decision as a married couple because we were leaving North Carolina and our college environs, moving to a large Northeastern city where we knew no one.

In the summer of 1970, we moved into a third-floor apartment in a beautiful Victorian brownstone in the historic downtown neighborhood of Bolton Hill. Robert had moved a month ahead of me to begin his job while I was still finishing the end of my school year as a teacher. I felt his emotional distance after I moved to Baltimore, but assumed he was preoccupied with his job at *The Sun*.

A few weeks after I joined him in Baltimore, he confided a shocking revelation. We were about to go to sleep one night when he told me he had a secret he needed to share. I was unsure what was coming because he was hesitant and looked worried, a bit frightened. We were lying together in our antique oak bed with the tall headboard, staring up at our 12-foot ceiling. I turned to look at him directly and quietly said, "What's that?" My heart raced, anticipating his words. I instantly thought he was going to tell me he was having an affair with another woman. Then he said, "I think I'm gay."

He didn't give any details about why he thought he might be gay or how long this had been on his mind. Nor did I ask. Initially, I was quiet and felt stunned by powerful, mixed emotions and confusion. Naively, I was relieved he wasn't having an affair with a woman. Still, I wondered how being gay was going to affect our marriage. "What does this mean?" I thought. "How can this be changed?"

I said to him softly: "Robert, you know I love you.... and we vowed to stay married to each other for the rest of our lives, 'in sickness and in health, till death do us part.'" Then I paused and said, "I think I've read that being gay might be a mental illness." He nodded in silence, with tears in his eyes, staring at the ceiling, not looking at me. I was in fix-it mode, so I cautiously added, "Maybe you need to see a psychiatrist who could help you with this."

In the face of my questionable reassurance and suggestion, he looked at me a bit dumbfounded. But what did I know? I had never heard of "homosexuality" until my college sociology course when I was required to read the Erving Goffman book *Stigma*.[2] And what did Robert know? Growing up in the South as a Southern Baptist, like me, he knew enough to want to hide, if not banish his urges. Perhaps marrying a Baptist preacher's kid served as good cover while he determined his sexuality. Robert must have felt some relief from my effort to respond with caring that night. Unlike our two previous years of marriage, we made love every night for a week. It was as though we were trying to disprove the legitimacy and permanency of his revelation. Surely, if we faked it, we could make it.

He didn't debate my recommendation and agreed it might be helpful to talk with a therapist. He didn't want to tell my parents—nor did I—but we casually knew a minister friend of my dad's in Baltimore whom we thought might help. He felt comfortable talking to this man to get a referral, and within a few weeks, he began what would be several years of therapy with a psychiatrist at Johns Hopkins Hospital. We rarely spoke again about his thoughts on being gay, nor did we talk about the progress of his treatment. I continued to wonder: "Is it working? Is he still gay?" Initially, it never crossed my mind to end our marriage, nor did Robert say he wanted out. His secret seemed to bind us together.

I never told another soul about that night, and Robert never told me how he managed his desires. My life of hiding his sexuality created a longing in me for a deeper sexual intimacy, which never came, and a longing for emotional intimacy with friends who did not know our marital secret. Nevertheless, for the next five years, we developed a solid community of close friends in Baltimore and built successful careers. I completed graduate school at

The University of Maryland, obtaining my master's degree in social work, like my father before me. Our son Michael was born a few months before I started my part-time master's program, and our daughter Sarah was born three years later, a month after I graduated. My MSW was sandwiched in between their births.

Robert and I bonded around co-parenting and supporting each other and our children through their early development and childhood illnesses. The challenges surrounding Sarah's health especially bound us close to each other. When she was born, she had severe hyperbilirubinemia caused by the breakdown of red blood cells, and she had to have a complete blood transfusion within a couple of days of her birth. Then, six weeks later, we awakened one morning to discover she had a fever of 106 degrees. We rushed her to the hospital, where she stayed for two weeks; she was finally diagnosed with a kidney infection and a congenital defect of double ureters, which caused reflux and the infection. During these health crises, Robert and I were united in caring for each other, as well as Michael and Sarah. He cared for Michael while I was in the hospital with Sarah since I was nursing her. We shared our fears and realized how important it was for us both to be involved in caring for our two young children.

In addition to co-parenting, we had fun exploring the city's antique stores and nearby countryside. We purchased and restored our first old home, a 3-story 1920 townhouse in the historical North Baltimore neighborhood of Oakenshawe. We bought a Shetland Sheepdog, trained her, bred her, watched her birth puppies, and gave one to my parents. We annually vacationed in the summertime at North Carolina's Outer Banks, joined by my parents, my sisters, and their families. Michael especially enjoyed flying kites and going fishing with his dad, his Uncle Rick, and my dad, known to the kids as "Deda."

We also found a church we liked in Baltimore and decided we were Episcopalians, a more affirming and accepting denomination than the Baptists. Together, we regularly attended Emmanuel Episcopal Church on Cathedral Street in the Mt. Vernon section of downtown Baltimore. At the time, the church had a liberal and intellectual atmosphere led by a rector whose sermons incorporated a philosophy of panentheism. This view proposed there is one God for all people, and the rector incorporated mysticism and other world religions into his sermons. Although we were not yet confirmed Episcopalians, we were drawn to this church and the denomination much more than the Southern Baptists. My faith was already in a stage of complexity, and the intellectual sermons preached at Emmanuel deepened the questions I had in college about Christianity.

On the surface, Robert and I had a rich and happy marital life, but our private life continued to hold secrets. We were close friends and loved each other, but in keeping with his preferences, we rarely talked about his sexuality.

Obviously, our sex life existed—we had two children—but it was less frequent than I would have liked. The lack of true intimacy in our marriage was never a topic of conversation. In graduate school, I was exposed to bio-psychosocial theories and research about human behavior, development, and psychopathology, which vastly expanded my understanding of sexuality, relationships, and family dynamics. That knowledge, plus Robert's sexuality and the lack of sexual intimacy in our marriage, pushed me from a stage of simplicity regarding sexuality to one of complexity.

I was privately questioning the quality of our marriage, realizing it did not have the level of sexual intimacy I wanted or needed. I was beginning to ponder how Robert became gay and whether it was something that could ever change. I also started wondering if he was having sexual relationships with men, though he never admitted to me that he was. In addition to my growing questions about our marriage—questions Robert and I rarely discussed—I had further questions about my faith. Sarah's health crisis and our exposure to our progressive Episcopal Church further deepened my doubts regarding my faith. I was no longer a compliant and unquestioning Baptist preacher's kid, trusting simple answers to my accumulating and complicated questions about sexuality and faith. Instead, I was falling into a deeper state of doubt.

Seven and a half years into our marriage, on Sarah's first birthday, we moved from Baltimore to Lexington, a small North Carolina town near Winston-Salem, so that

Robert could be the editor of the local newspaper, *The Lexington Gazette*, owned in those years by the *New York Times*. He was excited about this professional opportunity in his home state, but I was unclear where I fit into our new scenario. I felt sickened as we drove into the town with a population of about 10,000 and one Main Street. It brought back memories of my childhood in the small town of Red Springs, with its Belk's Department Store and Five & Dime on Main. This town, which claimed to be the "barbecue center of the world," starkly contrasted with the large city of Baltimore I had grown to love.

Our children were then one and four, and I needed to find a job to make ends meet. I soon began my first post-MSW position as a clinical social worker in the Neonatal Intensive Care Unit (NICU) of Baptist Hospital, a major teaching hospital in Winston-Salem affiliated with Wake Forest's Bowman Grey School of Medicine. An MSW whose own newborn infant was born with health problems, I was expected to work with the parents of critically ill babies in the NICU. My daily commute and two young children in full-time childcare strained our family life, so less than a year later, I quit my job to stay home with the children.

We also joined the local Episcopal Church, where we finally became confirmed Episcopalians and had our two children baptized. We made several good friends our age who had children similar in age to ours, and our social life immediately became quite active and vital to us as a family. We regularly socialized with these families and took a week-long vacation at the beach with them during our first year after moving. Our community of church friends enabled us to hide the unexpressed loneliness we both were feeling internally about our relationship.

As the Women's Movement and Gay Liberation Movement both gained prominence in American culture, we gradually recognized we were no longer a good fit for each other. It was 1977, and Anita Bryant, Florida's "orange juice queen" and Christian anti-gay activist, was spewing her message of hate against the gay community. As if in response, the Village People were celebrating gay pride with their popular hit songs, "Macho Man" and later "YMCA." The Gay Liberation Movement was in full swing, and gay people nationwide were becoming more open and vocal. During this time, Robert began to seem more distant and preoccupied, and about a year after moving, I began to intuit that he wanted to leave married life and live as an openly gay man.

In August of that year, I went to Carolina Beach with the children, two other women friends, and their children. Robert and I had no conversations that week apart, but I had a great time with my friends and all the kids. When I returned home from the beach, he was sitting alone on our large front porch in one of our four oak Kennedy rockers, deep in contemplation. Just looking at him, I knew. Our marriage was over. Without further explanation, I walked onto the porch while the children ran inside, looked at him intently, and said, "It's over, isn't it?" He looked at me without discussion and simply said, "Yes." It was as though our secret longings and concerns finally bubbled to the surface for us that week apart, enabling us to admit to each other and ourselves what we had privately known for a while. He wanted out of our marriage.

We spent the next three months in more open and intimate conversations about our marriage than we'd had in years, beginning with a brief stint of couple's therapy. The therapy served to confirm the marriage was over, and I realized I could not join him in his new life, though part of me wanted to. One day at home, when we talked about the future, I revealed my desperation when I asked Robert, "Do you think there's any way we could keep our marriage together by having a more open relationship?" Fortunately, he looked at me with love and kindly said, "Oh, Susanne, you would never be able to do that. And I would never do that to you or to us."

***

Over the next few months, I increasingly found my voice and clarity through my individual psychotherapy and writing in my journal. Robert also resumed individual treatment. Although I felt we still loved each other, I intellectually accepted that our marriage needed to end and that we needed to live separate lives. However, I emotionally held onto a simple and unrealistic fantasy that Robert's sexuality still might change someday. In December 1977, we signed documents to begin our formal, legal separation a little over nine years after our marriage began and seven years after he came out to me as gay. Robert moved that day into a rented house across the street from me to be near the children.

The day we signed the separation papers, I went alone to a big church party that night. By then, we had told our local friends we were separating without telling everyone why, and I felt they were supportive of us both. However, several men—married men from our church—hit on me during the party, noting I was now free and available. I was not flattered and instead began to feel I wanted and needed to get away from this group of people.

I finally shared with my longtime out-of-town friends and my sisters that Robert was gay, and that was the reason we were separating. Although I had known most of these people since before the day I married, I had never told them the reality of our marriage. It would be two more years before I felt comfortable sharing the truth with my parents, who had trouble understanding why we separated.

Grieving the end of our marriage, I initially experienced an assortment of emotions. I felt sorrow and fear about parenting our two and five-year-olds alone, anxiety about telling my parents the truth about our separation, and longing for Robert, who was still my best friend. And at the same time, I felt relief and excitement about my unknown future. I felt like a baby bird who had been pushed out of the nest but discovered she could fly. For a year, I felt no anger toward Robert because I had genuine compassion for him and knew that he could not change being gay. I also knew our separation and potential divorce was heartbreaking for him, as well as for me, because of his love for our children.

Within a few months, I felt drawn to leave our small town of Lexington due to Robert's prominence in the community as the newspaper editor. I wanted to shield our children from the stigma of growing up with an openly gay father in that Southern town, and I also sought to protect myself. I was troubled by the level of partying among my church friends and put off by the lack of boundaries I observed. Working with my therapist, I realized I needed to prioritize my well-being by relocating to a larger city where I could find better professional and social opportunities. Seven months after our separation, I moved with the children to Arlington, Virginia, hoping that Robert would also consider moving to the DC area.

On the way to Arlington, the children and I joined my parents, two sisters, and my brother-in-law at the Outer Banks for a week. We were at the Outer Banks for the first time without Robert. The weather was perfect, and the children had a great time with their grandparents, who doted on them. However, I felt so uncommunicative and morose that I spent the whole week alone in my bedroom or lying by myself on the beach. I was absorbed in reading a strange paperback beach book about Siamese twins. It was hard to imagine my life away from Robert, and I longed to feel connected to someone who truly knew me.

For Grief

By John O'Donohue

When you lose someone you love,
Your life becomes strange,
The ground beneath you gets fragile,
Your thoughts make your eyes unsure;
And some dead echo drags your voice down
Where words have no confidence.

Your heart has grown heavy with loss;
And though this loss has wounded others too,
No one knows what has been taken from you
When the silence of absence deepens.

—O'Donohue, J. (2008). *To bless the space between us: A book of blessings.* New York: Penguin Random House, pp. 117-118.

Five

Despair, Perplexity, and New Life

We grow spiritually by passing beyond some perfect Order,
through an often painful and seemingly unnecessary Disorder
to an enlightened Reorder or "resurrection."
This is the "pattern that connects."

—*Richard Rohr*[1]

With sole custody of the children, I moved to Northern Virginia to be near close college friends and start a new job in the District of Columbia. My friends assured me the public schools were better in the suburbs than DC, so I chose Arlington, Virginia as our new home. It was convenient—closer to Robert than Maryland and a manageable commute to my job in Northwest DC. Robert and I had discussed the possibility of him relocating to DC as well. In fact, he had brought it up before I ever considered moving, and that got me thinking about moving, too. I was determined not to be left behind in our small North Carolina town. Ultimately, Robert never moved.

My college roommate, who lived in the Maryland suburbs, helped me find a good job, a place to live, and a daycare center for Sarah. Our Arlington condominium was only a block from Michael's elementary school, where he was entering first grade, and it was a relatively short drive from the U.S. Capital. Since we lived close to the National Mall, I eagerly introduced Michael and Sarah to all the amazing and free Smithsonian museums. I hoped they would feel excited about this major life transition. While focusing on the adjustment and needs of my children, I worked hard to hide my secret nagging fears about our future. I even hung a framed quote on my kitchen wall: "Courage is when you don't let anyone know how afraid you are."

Michael and Sarah on the Mall in front of the Capital

Having landed from my leap of faith into the unknown, I was dizzy with excitement and fear, wobbly in my steps as I hesitated about where to go next. I was alone except for my children, who were anxious about moving and looked to me for direction. "Who will become our new friends?" they asked. "When will we see Daddy again?" Robert initially visited the children one weekend a month. When he came, he took them to a hotel for a long weekend, and they explored the city together. Over time, this was an expensive and unsustainable long-term arrangement, but he maintained steady communication with the children through phone calls, holiday visits, and regular summer vacations.

In February 1979, eight months after the children and I moved to Arlington, Robert and I signed our divorce papers. It was around this time that I started feeling anger toward him about our marriage ending because I was experiencing the challenges of caring for our children alone. Perhaps since I had lived with Robert for seven years while knowing his truth, sadness was initially more predominant than any anger. Denial, bargaining, and sorrow had consumed my feelings during our first year of separation, but anger arose when it was clear there was no hope of going back. My anger was entangled with my fears of financial insecurity, which consumed my thoughts. Although Robert regularly paid monthly child support, my salary as a social worker was meager. I had been inspired by the Women's Movement and, somewhat naively, felt compelled to be an independent woman, not dependent on my ex-husband for alimony. Eight months of living on my own with the children opened my eyes to the shortsightedness of that decision, which ultimately hurt us due to the reality of our family's limited finances. As I struggled to make ends meet, I was afraid for our future in this exciting but expensive city.

Loneliness also often overwhelmed me both at home and at work. After tucking the children into bed each night, I dreamed of my past relationships, former homes, and the joys of my previous supportive communities. I fantasized about the beauty of the maple trees blowing in the wind in our old front yard, the sound of the rain on our front porch tin roof, the reds and pinks of the Southern azaleas and tulips, and the ocean waves pounding the sand of our Outer Banks vacation cottages. I longed for the richness of my friendships with people I could no longer see or regularly hug. Although I knew my move was a sound decision for all of us, I deeply missed the life I left behind and the father of my little ones, now in my sole care.

⚜

Once in our new surroundings, I hungered for connection and a community to hold me up, to support the three of us so I could nurture my children, who looked to me for a sense of home. Having survived the move, held together by memories and hope, I shared my past and future dreams with strangers, hoping for their friendship. I made friends in my Fairlington Village condominium neighborhood with other mothers whose children were the age of my two.

I also made close friends at Children's Hospital National Medical Center in DC, where I became a social worker in the Neonatal Intensive Care Unit, a much larger NICU than the one in North Carolina where I first worked as a medical social worker. Affiliated with George Washington University's medical school, Children's NICU was nationally known, partially due to the prominence of the neonatologists who directed the NICU and the residency training program. Babies were not born at Children's, but the NICU was the regional care center for the most critically-ill high risk infants born elsewhere and flown by helicopter from hospitals throughout the wider DC-VA-MD metro area. This NICU also occasionally had babies flown from foreign countries because we were in the nation's Capital. One of two full-time MSWs in the NICU, I worked with the distraught and grieving parents of these infants, who were exceptionally ill due to life-threatening prematurity, illnesses, or congenital conditions.

My college roommate referred me to the job in the Children's NICU. She had recently worked at the hospital as a social worker before going on maternity leave and knew that Children's was hiring. Significantly, about a dozen social workers were hired that same year, and I became quite close with several of these women. I still count one of them among my closest friends today. In addition to beginning our jobs at the same time, most of the women in our group were working with families of children who were critically ill or were dying. We had much in common professionally and began meeting regularly with each other to provide mutual support about the challenges of our work.

While helping parents mourn the loss of their children, the group helped me reflect on memories of Sarah's birth and grieve the end of my marriage. My NICU experience evoked memories of the anxiety and fear I felt when Sarah was born with health problems. Although her illness was not as grave as that of the NICU infants, I could relate with empathy to the parents and their fears. My NICU work was further intensified and complicated by my active grief about my divorce. At times I felt overwhelmed and lost, wondering where God was amid so much loss. Parents in the NICU would share their anger, sorrow, and confusion about what it meant that their babies were dying, and they wondered if it was God's will or if they had failed. I too wondered what it meant for me that my marriage had died when I had been such a "good girl" and had tried so hard to have a family like the one I was raised in. In the 1970s, good Christian girls didn't get divorced, and at that time, I knew no one like me who was divorced and a single parent.

⁂

Eventually, I found a community of friends in St. Mark's Episcopal Church on Capitol Hill, which nurtured me and sustained us as a family for a decade. I was hopeful the first Sunday I drove with the children from Arlington to DC to visit St. Mark's, which my former North Carolina priest had recommended. Known as "St. Mark's Capitol Hill," the church had a reputation for being a progressive church that "welcomes doubters and nonbelievers," and I was excited to visit. The morning we first drove the eight miles from our Arlington home across the bridge into the city, we turned right to proceed up Independence Avenue, with the National Mall paralleling our route. I was struck by how beautiful DC is in the spring when there's no Sunday morning traffic and how quickly I could get into the city. As we drove up Independence, we soon passed the Botanical Gardens on our left, with the U.S. Capitol rising high in the sky just beyond it. Immediately behind the Capitol, we passed the stately, distinct Library of Congress building and turned left to see St. Mark's standing right behind the congressional library.

An impressive red brick building built in 1888, St. Mark's combined Gothic and Romanesque Revival architecture. It was a glorious spring day, with yellow forsythia blooming all around the church grounds. We walked into the side door and were warmly greeted by a woman, there with her daughter, the age of my daughter, Sarah. Like me, she was recently divorced and a new member of St. Mark's. She eagerly introduced us to several other families with young children.

When I walked into the large nave, I was awe-struck by the physical beauty of St. Mark's, which I later learned is on the historical registry. The nave had moveable chairs around a moveable altar in the center of the vast room, with a large cross hanging over the altar from the tall Cathedral ceiling. The walls were dark exposed brick—the same as the outside—with floor-to-ceiling-stained glass windows on two sides and a round Tiffany window at the back between the two front doors. I had never been in a church as dramatic as this one. It reminded me of pictures I had seen of European cathedrals, unlike the Baptist churches of my childhood. The unusual, serene beauty felt sacred, and the gracious welcome of the people we encountered that day confirmed I had found a church I wanted to join. I soon learned that most of St. Mark's members were young professionals close to my age, and we had similar religious doubts and political views. I felt I had found my folk.

St. Mark's had an active adult formation program nicknamed "Func Ed" for Functional Education. I immediately signed up for Func Ed's adult confirmation class, which met weekly for two hours over four months and included two weekend retreats at Rehoboth Beach in Delaware. In this class of about a dozen searching adults, we shared our life stories, admitted our spiritual questions, and pondered how God fit into our lived experiences. Slowly, at first, then eagerly, I became intimate with these new friends and experienced authentic, honest exchanges and longed-for acceptance. The children also made good friends at St. Mark's and participated in youth activities. Sarah became an acolyte and remained active until she left for college. Michael's involvement waned in early adolescence, but as a family, the three of us joined other St. Mark's families for church gatherings such as white-water rafting and camping in the nearby Shenandoah Mountains.

Through intense, personal small groups in the St. Mark's faith community, I began to feel the presence of the Holy Spirit within me, sustaining me amid my life struggles. I came to feel there was no one way to believe. Being straight or gay is not right or wrong, good or evil. Whether someone is Christian, Buddhist, or agnostic, faith does not have to be one way or another. Seeing the world through this expansive, inclusive, and connective lens became the theology that finally made the most sense to me. I experienced self-love, self-acceptance, and self-forgiveness. I let go of my shame of being divorced. I let go of my confusion and stigma of marrying a gay man, forgave him for my hurt, and accepted him for who he was and is. And, I removed the framed quote from my kitchen wall about not letting anyone know how afraid I was. I let go of hiding my fears and embraced a belief that real courage came from sharing my vulnerability with others. I experienced mutual love and acceptance from my family and new friends, and when we shared intimately, I felt the presence of the Divine.

I also returned to reading Paul Tillich and other contemporary theologians as part of my ongoing grieving process, seeking the link between my suffering and my faith. This time, I embraced Tillich for personal comfort rather than intellectual challenge. His words about the pain and the glory of being alone spoke to my heart. The Easter myth took on intense personal meaning for me for the first time: "There is no resurrection without death." I experienced a deeper faith as my divorce, which was the "death" of my marriage, led to a new beginning, and I felt hope unlike I had felt previously in life. As a child, I knew the Easter story and could recite the Bible's words. As a college religion major, I could analyze this Christian Easter story and compare it to myths in other world religions. But now I was experiencing the Easter story in a new way. The feeling of new life, *my* "resurrection," did not personally occur until I fully experienced the death of my marriage, the despair of my divorce, and the joy of the new life I was creating. That sense of new life came when I stopped debating literal interpretations of Biblical stories and church creeds and instead embraced the Gospel stories as metaphors for living my life.

⚶⚶⚶⚶

As I faced my post-divorce grief and doubts and embraced the love of the St. Mark's community, my faith evolved into McLaren's third stage of faith. Through a crisis of faith, the doorway from stage two faith moves a person into stage three, a faith of "perplexity." McLaren describes this phase of faith as "more than simple and more than complex: it is downright mysterious, downright perplexing."[2] People with perplexity faith are suspicious and skeptical. They appreciate the importance of viewing the changing context of situations rather than finding concrete, absolute answers. While they seek belonging, they stay on the margins or fringes of groups rather than the center of organizations. They also see God as a mysterious myth. A faith of perplexity is filled with doubts, where a person descends into the dark tunnel of unknowing, aware of how much they do not know. It is a stage where the skeptic may eventually emerge into mystical insight and contemplation and an awareness that God is present amid all doubts and despair.

In contrast to my college years, my faith became less intellectually academic and more personal and experiential. When my marriage ended, I was thrown into a crisis of faith about how I was going to manage life on my own and whether there was a God to sustain me in my struggles. After I moved to Arlington, my sorrow at times felt overwhelming. But when I began going to St. Mark's and sharing with kindred spirits in my small groups, I felt a mysterious lifting of my sadness and loneliness. By plunging into my despair, I began to feel joy on the other side, and the process was indeed perplexing yet hopeful.

During this faith phase of perplexity, I viewed God as a myth and mystery and the Bible as a collection of metaphors for daily living. Instead of relying solely on religious texts, I sought authentic relationships and embraced the struggles of my life to help me understand my questions about God and my faith. The adult formation classes at St. Mark's focused on recognizing the tensions of life dilemmas and proposed that we find God in these tensions, in the love present in our relationships, and in the metaphors for living that can be found in the scriptures. The death and resurrection story became the metaphor for my life's transformation.

In addition to my St. Mark's involvement during the decade of my 30s, I engaged in several years of psychotherapy and classic "on-the-couch" psychoanalysis four days a week. I explored my marital relationship and how my early childhood experiences shaped my marriage and current life. I completed a two-year adult psychotherapy training program and transitioned from practicing medical social work to practicing adult psychodynamic psychotherapy in a full-time private practice. I also intermittently dated men, trying to find someone who sparked my interest and fit with our family life. My female friends frequently set me up on blind dates, and occasionally, I formed brief relationships with men at St. Mark's. However, as a single parent of two school-age children, it was challenging for me to establish a meaningful relationship.

When dating, I came to realize that I was most drawn to men who were able to be intimate and open with their feelings and willing to engage deeply in conversations. In my late 30s, I had a brief romantic connection with a man who was a clinical psychologist, and that relationship affirmed for me that I am most attracted to men who can be as intimate and open as my female friends. I discovered those traits are hard to find in a man, though Robert had exhibited them in the earliest years of our relationship. Upon reflection, my sexuality was beginning to move into a stage of perplexity. I was no longer filled with questions about my marriage and why it ended. Instead, I felt mysteriously curious and perplexed about what characteristics truly attracted me to another person.

As I reached the end of my early adulthood, ten years after my divorce, I anticipated changes ahead. By then, both children were in their teens, and Michael had already started college. Working long hours as a full-time therapist in private practice, I wanted to change directions professionally. I was spending approximately 32 to 35 clinical hours a week doing intense psychotherapy with patients, many of whom were in long-term and complicated treatment. Although I loved my work, it had become quite draining. I began to fantasize about my life as an empty nester and how I might refocus my professional direction. I also was hopeful I might finally find romance once the children were both in college.

Part of me felt sad to see my children leave home, while another part was excited and hopeful about the inevitable changes and possibilities ahead. I felt God's presence holding me in this major life tension. I also felt comforted when I often listened to Judy Collins sing her melancholy song, "Everything Must Change." Its poignant themes of impermanence and the inevitable transitions of life resonated deeply, reminding me that change is a natural part of existence, and there is beauty in the unfolding mystery of it all. Little did I know then how much everything in my life would change once both my children became young adults, and I was clearly in my middle age.

Quotes from Paul Tillich

"Grace strikes us when we are in great pain...
Sometimes at that moment a wave of light breaks into
our darkness, and it is as though a voice were saying,
'You are accepted.'"
—Paul Tillich

"The courage to be is the courage to accept oneself, in
spite of being unacceptable."
—Paul Tillich

"Man's ultimate concern must be expressed symbolically,
because symbolic language alone is able to express the
ultimate."
—Paul Tillich

"Our language has wisely sensed these two sides of
man's being alone. It has created the word 'loneliness' to
express the pain of being alone. And it has created the
word 'solitude' to express the glory of being alone."
—Paul Tillich

—Tillich, P. (n.d). Top 25 quotes by Paul Tillich. Retrieved August
2024 from *A-Z Quotes* website.

Part Three

Middle Adulthood

Six

Changing Sexuality

Pain is important: how we evade it, how we succumb to it, how we deal with it, how we transcend it.

—Audre Lorde[1]

When I reached middle age, my life took an unexpected turn, and I changed directions regarding sexuality and relationships. Up to that point, my adult understanding of sexuality echoed the cultural messages of the 1950s and 60s, norms prevalent in the South in religious families like mine. As a preteen, I saw the 1956 newsreel videos of movie star Grace Kelly marrying Prince Rainier of Monaco, who captured her heart. These videos felt like the real-world version of the Cinderella fairy tale I read as a younger child, and they reinforced my daydreams about handsome men sweeping me off my feet. By the early 1960s, I was going steady with my high school boyfriend, and Rock Hudson was part of my fantasies; I didn't know in those days that he was a closeted gay man. Having a minister-father with a national reputation and an out-sized family influence further shaped my unconscious messages that a man should save and protect a woman. I wanted that when I married Robert and had remnants of those feelings when I reached middle age.

In my early 40s, I also still held many traditional notions about sexual orientation, gender, and gender roles internalized from childhood, although I had been married to a gay man. My sexual orientation was straight up until and during my 10-year marriage to Robert. Through years of psychotherapy and psychoanalysis that followed my divorce, I tried to understand why I married him. In all those years of therapy, I never questioned or doubted my sexual orientation. The therapy and professional training I had in my 30s primarily reinforced the inaccurate and homophobic views I had formed about sexuality. The essentialist messages coming from the Gay Liberation Movement stated that a person is born gay. In contrast, I embraced the psychoanalytic view at the time that sexuality was due to family dynamics or mental illness, not an inborn or unchangeable part of human nature. I thought I had sexuality all figured out until my children reached adolescence and began exploring their own sexuality. Then, my long-held views about sexuality began to fall apart.

⚜

When Sarah was still 17 and a senior in high school, she and I visited her brother for Christmas week in Paris. Michael had just turned 21 and was studying abroad at the Sorbonne in Paris during his junior year abroad, majoring in "postmodern studies." On Christmas Eve, the three of us stood on the plaza in front of the Notre Dame Cathedral at midnight, listening to the bells peal their loud pronouncement of Christmas Day's arrival. We stood beside each other amid crowds of holiday revelers, watching the exuberant joy around us. Sarah then proudly and spontaneously announced to Michael and me in her excited and confident voice: "I want you both to know that

I am definitely gay!" I felt tense and shocked, with my heart pounding and tears swelling. Michael promptly pulled the three of us into a shared embrace to celebrate Sarah's coming out, which she had been discerning for a while. I expressed support and joy for her, but privately, I felt emotionally shaken. I tried not to let her see my hesitation, but I worried about whether she would be accepted due to the stigma that people on the sexual margins of society sometimes experience. I held the belief that nurture carries weight over nature in the creation of sexuality, and I still minimized the role of genetics. I feared I had failed as her mother.

Fortunately, I had several professional colleagues and friends who were gay and lesbian psychotherapists, and they took me under their wings to re-educate me. They went to Lambda Rising, DC's gay bookstore in Dupont Circle, and bought me self-help books for parents of gay children and books for straight spouses with gay husbands or wives. Talking with these colleagues and reading voraciously, I became aware that my understanding of sexual orientation was both outdated and incorrect. I also learned how postmodern scholars consider sexuality and mental illness as social constructions, not in-born or family-caused problems. I decided it was time to pursue these interests, particularly since I was considering new professional directions once both children were in college. I explored various programs and became interested in Smith College's PhD program in social work. I hoped this degree would deepen my knowledge and qualify me to teach in academia for the remainder of my social work career. However, I became sidetracked on my way to meeting this goal.

When I initially talked with one of the co-directors of Smith's doctoral program to see if it would meet my needs and interests, she suggested I take summer continuing education courses on the Northampton, Massachusetts campus so I could gain a sense of Smith and what it would be like to live on campus. One of the two courses I decided to take was titled "Heterosexuality and Homosexuality in Women." Given all the conversations and reading I had undertaken the previous year, I was curious about the course content and looked forward to it. Although the course wasn't required for the doctoral program, I saw it as my first step toward preparing for my PhD in social work and focusing my dissertation research on the gay family.

On the first day of this course, we all sat around a large mahogany table in a windowless Smith conference room, and we each introduced ourselves. Half the dozen female students identified as lesbian and lived and worked in Northampton. I was the last person to give my introduction. Feeling embarrassed, I became tearful as I shared my story of being divorced from a gay man and the mother of a teen daughter who had recently come out. I didn't feel that I fit anywhere as a woman or a mother, and I wondered whether these women would accept me. My fears were unfounded as the group embraced me, and we continued to share our stories and study together during those two whirlwind weeks.

I also found connection and empathy with other students on the Smith campus that summer because I lived in the dorms to understand what being in the doctoral program might be like. Although I was a 46-year-old mother who hadn't slept in a college dorm room in 26 years, I found the experience refreshing. The mattresses weren't great, but the friendships I developed made dorm living worth it. One woman, a few years younger than I was, befriended me and captured my attention. Lesbian-identified and from New York City, Linda was a tall, lanky, curly-haired blond with blue eyes and a captivating smile and persona. She and I had thoughtful conversations about the content of the class I was taking, and she exhibited empathy for my life, charmed me with her humor, and made me laugh.

⚜

I was drawn to Linda's outgoing, warm personality and wanted to continue our friendship after our summer classes ended. When I prepared to leave Northampton and drive home to Arlington, knowing my route would take me through New York, I spontaneously asked her if I could spend the night at her apartment on my way home. With a smile and twinkle in her eyes, she said, "Sure, of course," without hesitation. As I followed her in my car from Northampton to her home in New York, I began wondering what I had gotten myself into.

That evening, we dressed up and taxied from her downtown apartment to an uptown exclusive Michelin-starred restaurant with incredible river views. The sparkling vista, the outstanding food, and the live jazz piano music played throughout the evening made the restaurant live up to its romantic reputation. However, the evening was most memorable because I became infatuated with my dinner date. I was emotionally drawn to Linda, who was funny, different, and magnetic. Her humor reminded me of my mother, and my newfound freedom and vulnerability left me uninhibited amid her charisma.

Over dinner, we spent the evening sharing details of our love lives. I heard her life story about being an out-lesbian since adolescence and being in many same-sex relationships. None of her relationships with women had lasted more than two years—a point I filed away in my mind. She listened with interest and empathy as I recounted stories about my high-school boyfriend, my husband, and my failed efforts to connect with men since my divorce. Our lives were profoundly different, but during our honest storytelling, we were mutually absorbed and warmly connected as we revealed more and more.

After dinner, we returned to her apartment, intoxicated by good wine and hours of intimate conversation about our lives. It was seductive to be so open with another person. I longed to be known, and there she was, eager to know me. Without forethought, I jumped into this new infatuation like an adolescent with a crush. Although I experienced Linda as flirtatious, she never took the lead with me that evening, respecting my boundaries and insistence that I was straight. When we were standing in her kitchen after dinner, fixing ourselves a drink, I was the one who first hesitantly said to her, "Would you mind if I kissed you?" She also hesitated but then responded. After our long kiss, she laughed and said, "Are you sure you're not lesbian?"

During the fun but turbulent next two years of our DC-to-NY long-distance relationship, I came to view my sexual identity in new ways. Linda taught me the ins and outs of lesbian relationships as she knew them and her views of how they differed from straight couples, though she had never been with a man. She also introduced me to New York City, and we explored the city and surrounding area as only residents know how to do it. I felt like an anthropologist learning a new culture—New York gay culture. As we came to know each other in more depth, however, it became clear that the 250-mile physical distance between us was minor compared to other distances. Our personality differences were significant, but our family, cultural, and religious differences eventually created an insurmountable expanse.

My time with Linda was the most chaotic period of my life. During the two years we dated, both my children were away in college, both my parents died, and I was living alone for the first time in my life. My weekend commute from DC to NY by train or car to see Linda threw me onto a physical and emotional rollercoaster. Her more infrequent train rides to DC were equally challenging. It became clear the long-distance nature of our relationship was exhausting and added complications for both of us.

Our weekends in New York began with excitement
and high romance and continued with fun adventures.
Most days, we walked around Manhattan and explored
neighborhoods and shops unique to the city, usually in the
East or West Village, Soho, China Town, or the Upper West
Side. We had bagels and lox from the coffee shop a block
away every morning, followed by lunch or dinner in
neighborhood diners, authentic ethnic restaurants, and
upscale cafes. Like many New Yorkers, Linda rarely
cooked. We often went to the theater for plays or films, and
sometimes, we traveled upstate to Woodstock and
Rhinebeck for a break from the city.

When she visited me, about half as often as I went to
NY, we toured the museums, the monuments, and the
parks. We ate out at restaurants, both the "cheap eats"
places and those with *Washingtonian Magazine* stars. She
was enthralled with DC and our life together when we were
there. One beautiful spring day, about nine months after we
met, I drove us along the George Washington Parkway
beside the Potomac to see the cherry blossoms across the
river. It was still early in the season, so the trees had not
fully bloomed, and traffic was light. We were on the
parkway between the Memorial Bridge and the Pentagon,
looking across the river at the Tidal Basin at trees just
opening their pink flowers. Linda suddenly said: "I think
we should get married—I want you to marry me!" I was so
shocked I nearly swerved off the road. At first, I was quiet
as I instantly thought, "Gay people can't marry, and
besides, I barely know you!" She noticed my hesitation and

how rattled I likely seemed, so I laughed and tried to make light of her question, unsure if she was joking. In hindsight, I think she felt hurt. Our busy weekend ended with her emotional withdrawal, which became routine in the weekly visits ahead. Her sullenness seemed related to facing another week of physical separation, but her moodiness left me hurt and confused.

"You are different from my other girlfriends," she sometimes said, questioning my sexual orientation and wondering why I was not like the "real lesbians" she had known and loved. She often said, "You are an emotional risk for me," because I had been married to a man, and she was my first lesbian girlfriend. She predicted our relationship would not last and worried how she would respond when it ended. Yet, despite her critiques, Linda seemed drawn to the challenge of being with me like a moth to a flame.

I was partly attracted to her because her life differed significantly from my suburban, single-parent lifestyle. However, I had no idea about gay culture or the norms for two women who were sexually coupled. I bought more self-help books from Lambda Rising about lesbian relationships to learn how to be Linda's "real lesbian." I wondered if I was really gay, and I continued to contemplate: "Are our problems due to my ambivalence and naivete? And why am I staying with her?" Her criticisms of me and her unpredictable moods began to feel emotionally abusive as we dealt with conflicts amid our mutual attraction.

As tensions grew and Linda's apprehension about me deepened, she moved from biting sarcasm to more substantial criticism. With fear and confusion, I once hid in her bathroom, frightened by our interactions. Behind the locked door, I called a friend to calm myself and gain perspective. I both needed and wanted to get out of this relationship, but I felt stuck and wondered what it would mean about me if I left. "Would it mean I'm not a lesbian, after all?" I asked myself. "If we love each other, shouldn't we be able to figure out how to make this work?" In hindsight, I still wonder why I stayed with her when I was so unhappy. Although Linda and I were both psychotherapists in private practice, with years of training and experience, we weren't applying our intellectual knowledge and professional skills to our private lives. We were unwilling to admit how much we were projecting our self-doubts onto each other.

I was facing additional challenges with my two young adult children as the three of us navigated my sexual transition. I felt they were trying to understand my surprising transition and its impact on our family dynamics. Sarah was 18 and trying to establish her separate identity when I first came out. I sensed she saw my transition imitating her life and that I was in her way and moving in on her tender new territory. Michael appeared to be coming to terms with being the only straight person in the family now that I had joined his father and sister by identifying as gay. I experienced my children's support in their separate ways, but I feared they were in some distress.

I felt conflicted and worried that I was no longer the predictable mother they had known.

In those years, I stopped attending St. Mark's, the church central to my life the previous decade. My faith and spirituality moved into the background of my mind, not because I thought I was sinning against God, but because I was absorbed with Linda and understanding my sexuality. The belief held by many religious groups, such as Southern Baptists and Catholics, was that being gay or lesbian was a sin. That view was not part of my vocabulary or my theology. Yet I wondered if my progressive Episcopal friends would accept the new me since they had known the old me in a completely different context. I also felt some embarrassment because these were the friends who had spent years fixing me up on blind dates with men. "What would they think of me now?" I wondered. After they knew about my transition, they seemed accepting, but I never felt at home at St. Mark's again. I was changing, and that change affected all my relationships.

As for my parents, they were understanding of Robert's sexuality once they finally learned he was gay, but I doubted they would feel the same about me. In the end, I never had to tell my dad because he suddenly died of a heart attack a few months after I began my relationship with Linda. I wrote him a private letter telling him about my transition, and I placed it inside his casket before he was buried. Somehow, I felt I was magically letting him know my truth. I did come out to my 73-year-old mother. Not surprisingly, she was shocked and distressed since she had known me as straight for 48 years. Still, Mom assured me that she loved me, and she accepted the situation as best she could. I appreciated how hard it was for her to adjust to her oldest daughter being a lesbian since I had just gone through that adjustment myself. She never knew Sarah also identified as a lesbian.

⊱⋆⊰

Shortly after coming out to her, and just 17 months after my father died, my mother was diagnosed with pancreatic cancer. I was completely shocked and had been in denial about her complaints of abdominal pain. All her CT scans and blood work had been negative, making me wonder if she was experiencing psychosomatic symptoms of grief about Dad's death. When her exploratory surgery revealed her abdomen was covered with cancer, I felt overwhelming sadness mixed with guilt that I had not believed her sooner. Mom was told there was no treatment for her incurable cancer. She was frightened and didn't want to be alone as she faced the end of her life. My sisters and I lived out of state, but we agreed to take turns with my Aunt Jane and Aunt Lily, who lived nearby, to stay with Mom in her home so someone would always be with her.

Within a week after Mom's diagnosis, Linda called me, and I was surprised to hear from her in the middle of the work week during the day. I was standing and looking out my living room window, talking to her on the phone when she suddenly admitted the reason for her call. "I've been thinking about it," she said. "I'm feeling ambivalent about being a part of your family's experience of caring for your mother while she dies." "What do you mean?" I asked, confused and noticing my throat tense up. Then she said, "I think we should end our romantic relationship." I felt like she was bailing out on me when I needed her the most, and I was surprised by her wish. I, too, had been thinking of ending our relationship, but I couldn't fathom breaking up with her while Mom was so ill. I needed to confide in someone about Mom and how I was coping. "Are you afraid of being reminded about the death of your own parents?" I asked. She concurred, and after much conversation, she agreed to continue to stand by me. Still, I felt unsettled and unsure I could trust she would be by my side in the months ahead.

After that phone call, Linda and I initially talked daily by phone, and sometimes, she was supportive, but other times, she was self-focused and distracted. Early in the summer, before Mom became overwhelmed with pain, I invited Linda to come to Louisville for the weekend to meet my mother. I thought it might be good for our relationship, and I also hoped Mom would feel more accepting of me if they met. Initially, Mom was ever the Southern hostess and welcomed Linda warmly into her home. Both extroverts, the two of them chatted comfortably, and the three of us felt relaxed together. Later in the afternoon, a friend of Mom's dropped by uninvited for a spontaneous visit to see how she was doing. When Mom looked out the window and saw this woman coming to the door, she rushed Linda and me to the back family room, told us to stay there until her friend left, and shut the door on us. Linda and I both laughed, realizing Mom's homophobia was causing her to hide us; she never would have acted that way under other circumstances. Linda didn't seem offended by it, but admittedly, I was embarrassed, disappointed, and hurt by Mom's behavior. Mom later acted like nothing had happened and returned to her friendly, engaging self the rest of the weekend.

After our Louisville visit, I saw Linda only once during the two remaining months of Mom's life. Taking breaks from my therapy practice, I spent several weeks that summer with my mother as she experienced increased pain and rapidly deteriorating health. During those weeks, I was deeply contemplating my spiritual beliefs about life and death, and I yearned to talk with someone who would listen to my family story, appreciate my religious background, and comfort me in my grief. Although I was close with my two younger sisters, we were each coping in different ways with Mom's illness due to differences in our personalities, our faith, and our unique relationships with our mother. It soon became clear by mid-summer that, although she had said she would stand by me, Linda also was not someone I could lean on.

At the beginning of August, Mom went into in-patient hospice, where she was bedridden and began taking higher doses of pain medications. Linda and I had a planned week-long vacation in Provincetown on Cape Cod the third week of August. Although Mom was nearing the end of her life, I didn't cancel our trip, but I should have. It was challenging for me to be with Linda because my preoccupation with my mother magnified the significant relationship problems Linda and I had developed—emotional distance, poor communication, and lack of mutual support.

During our week at the beach, I couldn't tolerate Linda's seeming indifference, and I coped by retreating into solitude with my private thoughts, thinking about my mother and her approaching death. I called Mom daily on the pay phone outside our beach cottage, even though she could barely talk. One day, when I felt rejected by Linda's emotional distance, I went alone for a long drive through the woods and stopped on a hilly bluff overlooking the ocean. Fortunately, no one was around to disturb me as I exited the car and sat, looking off at the ocean waves below my perch. I thought about my mom, remembering our conversations over the summer when I visited. Amid tears, I thought, "I long to be with you, Mom... I'm so blessed you've been my mother and were still there for me when I was with you this summer... forgive me for not being with you now."

As I sat and cried, I felt guilty being with Linda instead of my mother. I recalled my relationship with Mom throughout my life and missed being with her that week. My time with Mom that summer had helped me let go of my lingering sense that she didn't love me as much as my sisters. I didn't have the energy to talk with Linda about my complicated feelings and didn't trust she would understand or even care. She never once asked how I was feeling or where I had been when I went for that two-hour drive without her. Upon reflection, she and I were in completely different places, each of us having our needs unmet by the other.

When our beach week was over, I went straight to Louisville to spend several days with Mom, though by then, she was mainly unconscious on a morphine drip. Then, I flew home to Arlington to be with my daughter, who was about to leave for Latin America to study abroad for a year. On the morning of her departure that first week in September, we called Mom because we knew her life was near its end. Sarah and I snuggled in an overstuffed chair in our living room while I held her on my lap like a child. Both crying, we spoke on speaker phone with Mom, Sarah's "MeMaw," telling her goodbye and how much we loved her. Mom couldn't speak, but my sisters were in her Louisville hospice room and said she smiled and nodded her head with tears in her eyes while we talked. She heard us. She died an hour later. That afternoon, I drove Sarah to the airport to fly to El Salvador to begin her junior year abroad. Heartbroken and exhausted, I moved like a dazed robot to get through what I had to do in preparation for my mother's funeral.

The next day, I flew again to Louisville, this time for the funeral, held in the large St. Matthew's Baptist Church near Mom's home. I knew the church would be full because my parents were well-known, and it had been less than two years since Dad died. All our relatives planned to attend, and I wasn't sure how many knew of my relationship with Linda. My sisters had never met her, but they did know all about her. With some hesitation, I invited Linda to the funeral and paid for her plane fare. She didn't hesitate to accept the invitation, and despite my initial ambivalence, I was relieved she came. For two nights, she and I stayed at the nearby home of Dad's sister, Aunt Lily, who knew about our relationship and was a progressive and accepting woman. Although Linda and I had been stressed at the beach, our time in Louisville felt less awkward. Surprisingly, my connection with her at my aunt's house reminded me of the early months of our relationship. She was very loving and attentive, and I was thankful she had joined me for the funeral.

Hundreds of people, extended family, and out-of-town friends attended Mom's funeral, which was a joyful Christian celebration of her life. There were many Baptist hymns, a solo of "Amazing Grace," and a homily that brought laughter as we were reminded of Mom's funny antics, humor, and love of people. During the funeral, Linda sat with me and Michael, who had flown in from New York where he was now working. I sensed Linda felt uncomfortable and out of place. An unchurched person with no apparent spirituality, she had never been to a Christian funeral. I felt anxious having her meet family members who perhaps didn't know I was in a relationship with her. Fortunately, Aunt Lily was sensitive to our situation and was warm to us both. After the funeral, Michael, my sisters, cousins, and their families visited us at

Aunt Lily's house, and everyone seemed accepting of
Linda. I was relieved about my aunt's kindness and grateful
that Linda had come.

Linda and I never talked about what she thought of
the funeral and my family since she left early the following
morning to return home. The next time I saw her, which
was two weeks later in New York, I felt she was insensitive
to my grief. I needed her to hold me, let me cry, and
empathize with my feelings. I still wanted to hear how she
felt meeting my family and how she felt during the funeral,
but she was unable to meet my needs meaningfully.
Instead, she was initially lighthearted and excited to see me,
acting like the events of the past few months hadn't
happened. She wanted us to have a fun weekend, and she
insisted we go to an afternoon movie with her friend and
then out to dinner to boost my mood. I felt she was relieved
I was now free to devote my total attention to her.

When we left her apartment for the theater, I found
New York jarring due to the city's confusion, crowds, and
noises. I didn't realize how much that bothered me until I
sat watching a loud film in the dark movie theater. I needed
calm and comfort, not the chaos of New York that
surrounded me. The movie had started, but I whispered to
Linda how I was feeling, knowing I couldn't sit through
any film. I returned to her apartment while she watched the
film with her friend. A few hours later, Linda bounded into
the apartment and found me sitting alone on her sofa,

writing thank-you notes to the many people who had given my family flowers and had been present for us over the summer months.

Linda saw that the name on one of the envelopes was "Dr. and Mrs. Hicks," who were good friends of my parents. She immediately burst out laughing. She joked and said that the name was appropriate because most of the Southerners she had met at the funeral were "hicks." That was the final straw for me. My discomfort with her had been growing for at least half a year, but her insensitivity at this particular point in my life made me clear I wanted out of this relationship.

I stood up instantly in response to her insulting joke, quietly gathered up my notecards, and then looked at her and said: "You know... I can't believe you just said that... this relationship isn't working for me or us now, and I need to go home." She appeared surprised and stunned, but she didn't utter a word or attempt to stop me. Although I had just arrived in New York that morning, I quickly packed my belongings and left her apartment that late afternoon, rushing to catch the more expensive Acela train to DC. I was determined to go home as fast as possible.

Once home, I wrote her a carefully crafted, long letter about how I felt about our current and past relationship, writing what I could not say in person. I recounted positive memories of how we began our friendship and our fun times together the first few months of knowing each other. I expressed gratitude for our relationship over the past two years and admitted my part in its downfall, especially the challenges of living through my mother's death. She had warned how hard that would be, and she was right. I acknowledged I could not be the kind of girlfriend she wanted, nor could she be who I needed her to be. I was clear in my letter that our relationship was over. I mailed the letter by priority mail and wondered if she would respond.

I didn't hear from Linda for almost two weeks when she called me one night, begging me to come to New York "immediately" because she was "sick" and was in the hospital emergency room with unexplainable symptoms. She sounded angry and frightened. "You're my girlfriend. I need you, and you must come to me now!" she forcefully insisted. We talked briefly, long enough for me to hear details about her symptoms and that she had her friends with her in the ER to help. She didn't mention my letter, so I reminded her I sent it and repeated what the letter had said: "Our relationship is over, Linda, and I'm no longer your girlfriend." And I added with emphasis, though I tried to sound compassionate, "I'm truly sorry you're sick, but I'm not coming." I was scared of being sucked into taking care of her, whatever her illness turned out to be. It was too late for me, especially after all that I experienced over the summer while my mother was dying. John O'Donohue[2] writes in his blessing about grief, "Flickers of guilt kindle regret, for all that was left unsaid or undone." For months, part of me regretted and felt guilty about how I ended my relationship with Linda and how much was left unsaid and undone. Yet another part of me knew our relationship had ended, and I was certain I wanted it to end.

❦

My relationship with Linda began with blind infatuation, in a stage of sexuality that could only be described as simplistic. A friend who knew us recalls how passionate I was about Linda and that I had no initial questions or doubts about what I was doing or experiencing. I was "all in" the relationship. Perhaps that's how many people feel when they are initially infatuated with another person, but, in my case, it felt more dramatic since I was experiencing my first sexual infatuation with a woman.

However, in less than a year, doubts arose for me, and our relationship became complicated. My sexuality moved from a stage of simplicity to one of complexity. I was confused by the variations in Linda's mood and questioned the quality of our relationship. I thought our relationship was not the one I wanted. I did not question my attraction to Linda because she was a woman; instead, I was doubtful she was the right woman for me. The death of my mother was the crisis that initiated my transition from one of complexity into a new phase of confusion regarding my sexuality. I spent the next several years in a stage of perplexity, pondering my sexual fluidity and what it meant for my life and exploring the origins of sexual orientation and gender as part of human development. I also spent months grieving my triple loss—the death of my mother, the absence of my daughter for a year abroad, and the end of a significant romantic relationship, all occurring within a few weeks.

⸺✦⸺

Four years later, I was in New York for work. Being in the city again made me feel drawn to contact Linda to see if she was interested in seeing me and sharing any unfinished business about our time together. She was surprised to hear from me but was curious, so we met at a diner we had frequented years earlier. We laughed about how we both had aged and put on weight, and we updated each other on mutual acquaintances and changes in our professional lives. We talked briefly about our previous relationship, and it was clear we both had let go of past regrets or hard feelings. We both had moved on.

Interestingly, toward the end of our lunch, she looked at me with her cocked head and her flirtatious smile, and she winked. For a brief moment, the powerful mutual attraction between us emerged again. We smiled knowingly at each other and seemed to both feel the connection. I knew the feelings I once had for her were real, but the relationship was over. After that day, I never saw Linda again.

For One Who Is Exhausted

By John O'Donohue

The tide you never valued has gone out.
And you are marooned on unsure ground.
Something within you has closed down;
And you cannot push yourself back to life.

You have been forced to enter empty time.
The desire that drove you has relinquished.
There is nothing else to do now but rest
And patiently learn to receive the self
You have forsaken in the race of days.

At first your thinking will darken
And sadness take over like listless weather.
The flow of unwept tears will frighten you.
You have traveled too fast over false ground;
Now your soul has come to take you back.

—O'Donohue, J. (2008). *To bless the space between us: A book of blessings.*
New York: Penguin Random House, pp. 125-126.

Seven

Graduate Education Perplexity

Revelation lives in paradox;
understanding, as opposed to knowing,
thrives in unknowing;
and welcomeness and belonging
thrive in my continual becoming.

—*Cassidy Hall*[1]

After ending my troubled relationship with Linda, I felt relieved and free from the chaos of the previous two years. Yet, I also felt confused about who I was and what this previous relationship meant for my future. I was mourning the death of my parents, and the loss of my romantic relationship complicated my grief since both my parents died during the two years Linda and I were together. Fortunately, I had a robust support system composed of my sisters and several close women friends who were psychotherapists. They all had met Linda and were able to provide me with empathy, love, and wise counsel. My sisters and I were also in frequent contact as we settled our parents' affairs, sold our family home in Louisville, and spent our holidays together the year after Mom's death.

Nine months after my relationship with Linda ended, I returned to Smith College in Northampton. It was there, three years earlier, that I had first met Linda while I completed my continuing education courses. This time, I was committed to obtaining my PhD in social work, hoping to deepen my understanding of gay families, as well as my own sexuality, while also enhancing my professional skills and credentials. Inspired by my father's professional achievements, I had wanted to obtain a doctorate for many years. After Robert and I divorced, I fantasized about moving to New York to study psychology and religion at Union Seminary, combining my two primary academic interests and following in the footsteps of my college professor, Dr. Trible, who was then a Union professor. I even went so far as to visit the school and talk with faculty, which made me realize I could not manage the program financially or logistically as a single parent of two elementary-age children. I postponed my dream of higher education until my children were in college. After the death of my parents, I finally had the financial means, time, and space to undertake advanced studies and move toward a career in academia.

Nationally acclaimed, Smith was the ideal graduate program for me due to its psychodynamic and relational approach to clinical practice and its emphasis on social justice as well as racial and cultural diversity. The program's academic focus and mission aligned with my experience, interests, and values. The program was also feasible because it had a block curriculum. Coursework was concentrated over three summers on campus, with a home-based supervised internship in the intervening months. This arrangement allowed me to maintain my private practice to help pay for my education. Over the next five years, I focused on gay families, self and relational theories, attachment theory, and research.

Arriving on campus in June 1996, I lived with most of the doctoral students in Caldwell Hall, a large, multistoried, turn-of-the-20th-century brick house. It had a massive

living room with a grand piano, a front porch complete
with a porch swing, large bedrooms with 12-foot ceilings
and tall windows, shared bathrooms, and small kitchens on
each floor. Across the street from the dining hall and the
main campus, Caldwell became a favorite gathering place
for our cohort of 12 diverse students. We had a wealth of
professional experience, and our ages ranged from early 30s
to early 50s. At age 49, I was the second oldest student in
my class. Predominantly women, my cohort hailed from all
over the country, from the West Coast and Middle America
to the Mid-Atlantic and New England—all cis-gendered
people who identified as straight, lesbian, gay, or bisexual.
Racially, we identified as white, Black, Indigenous, Filipino,
and Latina. Religiously, we were Protestant, Catholic,
Jewish, or "none." We laughed in amazement about how
the Smith admissions committee must have purposefully
selected us to be the most diverse class of social workers
they could find that year. We lived, ate, and studied
together. We were in the same courses seven hours a day,
four days a week, for ten weeks. I welcomed the rich
diversity in my cohort and soon realized how much we
learned from each other amid our intense academic and
cultural immersion.

The first week, I felt a mixture of emotions. I was
excited when I arrived on campus and met my new
classmates, people I would come to know intimately in the
weeks ahead. I was anxious about the program's
challenging academic expectations. The amount of reading
was overwhelming, and writing major papers every week

seemed an impossible expectation. In addition to my grief and continuing confusion about my sexuality, I had conflicted feelings about the privilege of attending Smith, which was only financially possible because of my parents' deaths and my subsequent inheritance. I knew I needed to return to therapy to have someone help me sort through these emotions so I could concentrate on my studies.

I met with the co-chair of my doctoral program and shared my mixed emotions. She referred me to a private psychotherapist in Northampton, a clinical social worker and well-known author specializing in lesbian families. I began seeing her during the second week and soon realized she was the most empathic and effective therapist I had seen in all my previous years of psychotherapy and analysis. I poured out my story in my first session, talking and crying continuously throughout that whole first hour. She never said a word or questioned me; instead, I felt her deep empathy as she looked at me intently, nodding her encouragement, and never interrupted my desperate need to talk. It was exactly what I needed to do. I saw her twice a week during my 10-week summers at Smith and then continued to work with her by phone for several years after I completed my residency, conducted my research, and wrote my dissertation.

During my years of work with this therapist, I processed my grief over the death of my parents, the end of my relationship with Linda, and the transition in my sexual orientation. Letting go of being straight felt like a loss. In therapy, I asked myself: "What did the past three years mean? I never would have put up with a man treating me like Linda did. Why did I let it happen?" I also wondered, "Who am I anyway? Am I truly gay?" My therapy helped me clarify the sexuality of my younger years, just as I had outgrown my childhood religious beliefs when I was in college. I realized I was evolving sexually, similar to how I evolved spiritually the decade after my divorce. My aging process, ongoing education, and insatiable search for meaning in life found me replaying Judy Collins' voice repeatedly in my mind as she sang about the inevitability of everything changing over time as we age.

⚶

In addition to research and social policy classes, much of Smith's required curriculum focused on classical psychoanalytic and contemporary relational theories that I could apply professionally and personally. In my clinical relationships, I focused on recognizing and working with transference (my client's feelings about others redirected onto me) and countertransference (my feelings redirected toward my clients). This work helped me understand some of the dynamics of my earlier relationships, the pull of empathy toward Robert, the conflict and criticism with Linda, and my role in our interactions.

Among the range of theories we learned, I was particularly drawn to the work of Donald Winnicott,[2] a well-known English psychoanalyst and child pediatrician during the mid-twentieth century. After my years of

123

working in the NICU at Children's Hospital and my own positive experiences of motherhood, Winnicott's theories of infant development and the mother-child relationship resonated with me. Through his observations of young children, he penned poetic and beautifully written works that introduced theories now incorporated in clinical practice with both children and adults. He was also the first scholar to develop a theory about the *true self and false self*, concepts adopted in the work of spiritual writers, such as Thomas Merton[3] and Richard Rohr.[4] Winnicott suggested that infants are born with an authentic, spontaneous, true self and that the quality of the relationship between infants and their primary caregivers is vital to the young child's emotional development. An authentic true self develops when parents provide a safe and attuned holding environment to meet the infant's needs.

I intuitively understood Winnicott's theories. I was fortunate to have had that sense of safety in my childhood and had tried to provide it to my children. When my two children were infants, I would gaze into their eyes, smile lovingly, and watch them smile back. By reflecting and mirroring their happy moods and expressions, I conveyed that I saw them, was awe-struck by them, and loved them. When either of them were upset and crying, I would hold and comfort them, mirror their expressions, and remain attuned to their distress. This further reinforced that I saw them and was providing an environment that enabled them to be themselves. Even when they were upset and crying, they were supported. As challenging as it would be some days, I would hold my babies against my chest as I strolled around the room, empathizing with their pains, hoping my soothing voice would settle them down. Winnicott proposed that this quality of interaction is crucial to developing a child's *true self.*

Parents who fail to respond or ignore the needs of their young children send a message of misunderstanding and misattunement. In response, these children try to develop ways to gain parental attention or soothe themselves without the comfort of a loving adult. These children may become people-pleasers to get approval, or, in contrast, they may act out to get attention. When older, they may engage in self-harmful behaviors to soothe themselves and hide their pain. Over time, these children create a *false self* that conceals how they genuinely feel inside.

Applying Winnicott's ideas of true and false self to my clinical work, I practiced mirroring my clients' expressions and how they presented themselves. I listened deeply to their concerns and how they felt misunderstood and hid their true selves from others to gain approval. Over time, as they began to trust they could be authentic in their conversations with me, they revealed their more profound wishes and authentic selves. I saw that mirroring, accepting, and supporting a person's true self is vital to recovery for most people in therapy. I also realized that my current therapist was relating to me in this manner, and it worked. The more I felt her empathy and acceptance of my feelings, the more my hurt from past losses disappeared. Our loving, relational connection was the key to healing my wounds, building my self-acceptance, and affirming my true self. I tried to mirror my clients the way I experienced my therapist mirroring me, creating Winnicott's attuned holding environment.

⸻

Smith required doctoral students to complete a supervised clinical internship interspersed between three residential summers of coursework. I chose to do my internship at DC's Whitman-Walker Clinic. At that time, Whitman-Walker was the only agency in the metro area that focused on treating gay and lesbian clients, providing health care for people living with AIDS, and mental health care for the LGBTQIA+ community. While continuing my private practice, I worked at the Arlington branch of Whitman-Walker two days a week, providing psychotherapy to lesbian and gay clients. The AIDS epidemic was still prevalent, although the pharmaceutical "cocktail" that eventually became effective had just become available. During my clinical work, I provided intense twice-a-week therapy for gay men living with AIDS and gay and lesbian individuals seeking support from a welcoming, gay-affirming therapist. Through this experience, I gained a deeper understanding and empathy for the lifelong stigma and shame many of my clients described.

In addition to our coursework and internship, Smith required us to meet a research requirement of participating in another person's research project. Previously, I had been a clinician in practice for over 20 years and had no contact with the research world. I knew I would need to reach out to someone to meet this research requirement. In my first few weeks at Smith, I became familiar with the work of a developmental psychologist who was nationally known and was conducting research on children of lesbian families, which was just what interested me.[5] I boldly called her and asked if I could work with her. She was welcoming and invited me to work on a research study she was conducting on adoptive lesbian parents. I began doing research for her by interviewing lesbian couples in Northampton who had adopted children.

This research internship proved helpful as I began thinking about my dissertation. After finishing my research internship, my Whitman-Walker clinical internship, and my three summers of coursework, my dissertation was the final requirement for my doctorate. Before attending Smith, I had wanted to study gay and lesbian families. In keeping with the adage that "all research is me-search," I had considered researching families like mine, exploring how biological children are affected developmentally by having gay parents. This soon felt a little too close to home, increasing the risk of bias in my research. I decided that lesbian adoptive couples, like the ones I had interviewed for my research internship, would be a better population focus for my dissertation. I decided to interview parents who had adopted internationally, which was a growing phenomenon at that time.

My research was timely in that the 1990s was the era of the "lesbian baby boom." Hundreds of lesbian couples were creating new versions of family life by having children through artificial insemination or international adoption.[6] I was interested in exploring attachment processes in lesbian families because theories about attachment had been based on the relationships in heterosexual families and made assumptions that the mom was the primary parent. I wondered about the usefulness of attachment theory in non-traditional families.

I first became familiar with attachment theory when I was a clinical social worker in the NICU and witnessed the profound grief and separation anxiety experienced by parents when their newborns were in intensive care with life-threatening conditions. I remembered the powerful feelings Robert and I had when Sarah was an infant and critically ill. I also was interested in attachment theory because it helped me understand my family dynamics. I knew I was blessed to be raised in my family, where I felt secure with both parents and had internalized that secure attachment. Yet, I was curious about the different degrees of security I felt in my relationships with Mom and Dad. What had made that difference, and why did I feel more secure with my father, who, I realized, was my primary attachment figure? These personal and professional experiences motivated me to focus on attachment theory for my dissertation research. In addition, I knew attachment theory would be critical to understanding these adoptive families.

Built on the work of John Bowlby and Mary Ainsworth,[7] attachment theory proposes that humans are social creatures with natural, inherent needs for intimate connections with others. Individuals who provide safety, security, and a sense of belonging are known as *attachment figures*. Theoretically, an infant develops an attachment bond to one primary attachment figure, although the child has other secondary attachment bonds, creating a *hierarchy of attachments*. Attachment security is the internalization that one is loved, and one's attachment figure provides a refuge whenever needed. When young children are securely attached, they develop their true selves and a sense of security that gives them the confidence to explore the world beyond the *secure base* of their attachment figure. When exploration is temporarily shut down due to fear or anxiety, the child returns to the *safe haven* of the attachment figure until security is restored and the child feels sufficiently secure to explore once more.

My dissertation study examined these attachment processes in lesbian co-parent families with internationally adopted children, exploring the question: "Who is the Primary Mom?"[8] I interviewed 30 mothers (in 15 couples) about their experiences adopting their children and their perceptions of the parent-child attachments in their families. I was curious if a newly adopted child would develop a primary attachment bond to one parent over the other since there were two maternal caregivers and neither mother had a biological tie to the child. If that happened, what created the attachment hierarchy? My study's findings suggested that all the children in these families developed attachments to both their mothers, but in 12 of the 15 families, the child developed a primary bond with one of the mothers. The mothers told me they shared parenting and division of labor, but there were differences in how they interacted emotionally with their children. The quality of caregiving appeared to be the primary factor that created the child's attachment bond in these families, rather than the amount of time the mother spent with the child.

My study was significant because it suggested that the same attachment processes that exist in straight families with biological children exist in adoptive families with two moms. In other words, family structure doesn't prevent or cause the creation of attachment for the child. The findings also suggested that the quality of the emotional connection between mother and child, not the time spent with the child, leads to the primary attachment. That finding didn't surprise me, but it was a sensitive point for some lesbian couples I interviewed who resisted the idea that either mom was primary in their homes.

These findings also made me reflect on my relationships with my own parents. Although Mom was loving, warm, and fun, I felt Dad had more empathy for me. As a young child, I always turned to him instead of her when I was troubled, afraid, or needed support. I felt securely attached to both of them, but he was my primary parent.

Completing this research study was a massive undertaking, considering the time involved and the emotional and intellectual energy required. The process not only shaped my professional focus, it also influenced me personally in some essential ways. When I began the program, although a long-held dream, I was concerned about whether I could manage the demands of the curriculum, given my age and insecurity about my academic abilities. My self-confidence grew as I immersed myself in my studies and received positive feedback. Innumerable rich relationships with my lesbian therapist, my lesbian and gay classmates, clients, and professors, plus the dozens of in-depth interviews I conducted with lesbian moms, all helped me develop clarity about my sexuality. I had entered the program with questions and much confusion about my sexual self and my relationship with Linda. Therapy helped me navigate this full-blown stage of perplexity regarding my sexuality, grief, and all the emotional turmoil I felt at that time. By the time I graduated, I realized the breadth and depth of what I had learned and how it had changed me.

⚜

McLaren suggests that a stage of perplexity for faith development is moving into a tunnel of unknowing, of realizing how much you do not know.[9] When I started my doctoral program, I was still in a stage of perplexity about my faith, but I also was in a tunnel of unknowing regarding my sexuality. I was confused by reading postmodern literature about sexuality and sexual fluidity, as well as

Freudian psychoanalytic literature about sexual development and relationships. Rather than answering my many questions, the material presented contrasting viewpoints and left me unclear on how sexual orientation develops in general and uncertain about the formation of my sexuality. My critical thinking skills were challenged as I tried to make sense of these conflicting perspectives.

Integrating my studies with my personal experience, I eventually came to believe that an individual's sexuality may change if they are open to the possibility of change, as I always have been. However, no amount of psychotherapy or religious intervention, such as "conversion therapy," can change, cure, or heal one's sexuality. I believe my sexuality was influenced, though not created, by my exposure to my husband's sexual identity and my education about LGBTQIA+ individuals and culture, which made me both open and curious. After much study and consideration, by the time I finished Smith, I concluded that sexual orientation has a genetic component for many people. Still, that component is not always straightforward or predetermined.

I do *not* believe that sexuality is solely determined by genetics, *nor* do I think it is exclusively a conscious choice. Instead, a person's sexuality and gender are shaped by many factors, including genetics and hormones, culture and society, religious background, family dynamics, and interpersonal relationships. Sexual orientation and gender also exist on a spectrum, and they can be fluid and nonbinary, particularly for women who fall somewhere in the middle of the spectrum. Research psychologist Lisa Diamond has written, "One of the fundamental, defining features of female sexuality is its fluidity."[10] I now know that I am someone who falls in the middle range of the sexual orientation spectrum and that my sexuality is fluid.

My life story about sexuality does not make sense to some people, and it once did not make sense to me. Some straight men I dated wondered how I made my husband gay, as though it was my fault. Some straight women have expressed confusion about how I could be attracted to men until middle age and then attracted to women. Some lesbians who have been sexually attracted to women all their lives have challenged me, insisting I must have been in denial when I was young and did not know myself. How could I be married to a gay man for ten years yet be straight? Sometimes, I wonder if these questions stem from a lack of understanding about sexuality, especially women's sexual fluidity. Or perhaps, for others, these questions reveal anxiety as they try to imagine a life story that is so different from their own or fear that their life could similarly and unexpectedly change.

Despite the doubts of others and doubts I once had about myself, I know I was genuinely attracted and sexually aroused by my high school steady boyfriend, my husband, and several men I dated after I was divorced. Eventually, when my children left home, I felt free to experiment and curious about same-sex relationships, in part because Sarah had come out. Some people have mistakenly labeled me bisexual, but it is more accurate to say my sexuality is fluid, and I transitioned to being with women in middle age when I met a woman who sparked my sexual interest. I was strongly attracted to Linda and then two other women I dated after her. After being with women for over 32 years, I can no longer imagine being with a man, just as I could not imagine being with a woman until I was.

Whether with men or women, I have been sexually attracted by a combination of characteristics, not simply the looks, biological sex, or gender of the person. The romantic spark strikes me most when I feel a physical and erotic attraction to someone who energizes and enlivens me, brings me pleasure and joy, and makes me feel understood, respected, and eventually loved. Characteristics of my parents also play a role in my attraction, such as their empathy, warmth, humor, intelligence, and acceptance.

After five years, I emerged from my tunnel of uncertainty about my sexuality, guided by my unwavering trust in the rigorous scholarly journey of my education at Smith. I am grateful for the knowledge I gained and the relationships I experienced along the way because they helped me clarify and solidify my sexuality and my sense of self, both personally and professionally. My classes, readings, internships, and research gave me extensive academic knowledge. Intimate relationships with my diverse classmates widened my worldview, and my relationship with my empathic therapist deepened my emotional intelligence. I finished the program hopeful about developing an academic career, and I was finally clear about myself sexually. When I graduated in 2001, I realized my time at Smith had been the most transformative five years of my professional and personal adult life.

A Prayer for Unknowing

My Lord God,
I have no idea where I am going.
I do not see the road ahead of me.
I cannot know for certain where it will end.

Therefore will I trust you always though
I may seem to be lost and in the shadow of death.

I will not fear, for you are ever with me,
and you will never leave me to face my perils alone.

—Merton, T. (1956/1958). *Thoughts in Solitude.*
The Abbey of Our Lady of Gethsemani.

Eight

New Marital Commitment

Unfurl yourself into the grace of beginning
That is at one with your life's desire.

—*John O'Donohue*[1]

I met Cheryl one month before I graduated from Smith
and eight years to the month after I first met Linda. My
relationship luck had not been positive since coming out, so
I wasn't optimistic about our planned blind date arranged
by our mutual friend, Anne. Cheryl and I were both
pleasantly surprised as we chatted easily over Middle
Eastern food in a Bethesda Row restaurant. A friendly,
feminine, and pretty woman with summer-tanned skin,
dark brown eyes, and short sandy-colored hair, Cheryl
seemed familiar, like straight women friends I had known
for years. Although ten years older than I, she was vibrant
and appeared much younger than her age. We both later
laughed and admitted how relieved we were when we first
saw each other. After finishing dinner and parting ways
with Anne, we continued talking over coffee for hours at a
nearby Barnes & Noble until it closed.

Sharing our stories and life histories, we discovered
we felt comfortable with each other and were both
interested in knowing more. Our life experiences were
sufficiently different to create curiosity and excitement, so
we both wanted to develop our friendship. Cheryl is warm
and empathic, a good listener and understanding, well-
educated and highly intelligent—all characteristics that
sparked my interest and are essential to me in a romantic

relationship. Looking back, I see that we were inevitably drawn to each other because we have much in common, though we have very different personalities and experiences.

Cheryl and I both grew up in the South, in families with educated and professional parents we admired. We were previously married to men we loved—she had been widowed for 13 years from her husband John—and we each had two adult children from those relationships. We were surprised when we realized that both John and Robert began their professional careers as journalists. We shared the same political and religious views and were both practicing psychotherapists with similar training and education. What made our bond even stronger was the fact that we transitioned sexually in our middle age years and had young adult daughters who identified as lesbians. These specific traits made us feel we had more in common with each other than any other women we had met. I felt she understood and accepted me better than anyone I knew. We soon developed an easy, genuine friendship that eventually grew into a romance, but we did not exemplify the tired joke that lesbian couples hire U-hauls as soon as they meet. Instead, it was two years before we started living together.

We quickly realized how our adult life experiences and personalities differed, making our relationship more interesting than challenging. My life as a single parent and a recent five-year doctoral student contrasted considerably with her life, which included extensive travel due to work and marriage. I enjoyed listening to stories about her family's decade in Latin America when John was in the U.S. Foreign Service. Cheryl had three master's degrees—one in anatomy/physiology, one in counseling, and one in social work. She had previously worked as a counselor and head of training for a student exchange organization, enabling her additional international travel. Regarding our personalities, Cheryl was more reserved, cautious, and introverted than I, while I tended to be more spontaneous and outgoing, often taking the lead on activities or decisions. She benefited from my willingness to act, while I benefited from her good judgment in slowing down and making thoughtful decisions.

In our first year together, we met each other's friends and began to blend our lives. We both had lived in the DC area for decades, though our paths had not crossed. I lived in Virginia, she lived in Maryland, and the Potomac River flowed between us. We began to socialize as a couple with our respective friends, surprised at how many people we knew in common. Cheryl had a memorable dinner party at her house about six weeks after we met to introduce me to her best friends at her church, St. Alban's Episcopal in DC. Our mutual friend and colleague, Anne, who had been our matchmaker, was the only dinner guest I knew. That evening, I met Julia, the Associate Rector at St. Alban's; Julia's wife, Carly; Cheryl's best friend, Josie; and her husband, Rich. That evening, full of laughter and intimate storytelling, Cheryl and I felt a deeper connection to each other through sharing our spiritual histories.

As I told Cheryl's friends about my childhood of being a Baptist preacher's kid, followed by my profound spiritual renewal at St. Mark's after my marriage and divorce, I began to cry. My tears stemmed from the relief of being authentic and intimate, feeling understood and accepted by these new friends. Julia reached over and patted my hand while I shared my story, signaling her compassion and empathy. That night, I became aware of how much I longed to be with people who could understand and accept my complicated life story of an evolving faith, of being married to a gay man, and of transitioning sexually in my middle age. I sought a life partner who, like me, was on a spiritual journey and understood sexual fluidity, marriage to a man, and motherhood. That night, I realized I finally had found someone—and a chosen family of friends—where I could truly belong. That night, I felt the first arousal of falling in love again.

⁂

Despite that intimate evening, or perhaps because of it, I began to feel anxious about being with Cheryl. In my eight years of identifying as lesbian, Cheryl was the first woman I dated who truly understood and accepted me. I was afraid a romantic connection might not last—none of my other relationships had—and then I would lose her as a friend. At this age, having a friend like Cheryl mattered more to me than having a romance. The following week, I admitted my hesitation to her, so we spent the next couple of months just "hanging out"— going to movies, out to dinner, socializing with friends, but nothing more. Slowing down the development of our relationship was just what I needed, and the more Cheryl responded to me as "just a new friend," the more at ease I felt and the more romantically interested in her I became.

However, when she spent Thanksgiving that fall with her daughter and her family on Cape Cod, I became concerned about the possibility of any future with Cheryl. That holiday weekend, she spontaneously bought a second home in the picturesque town of Brewster on the bay side of "lower" Cape Cod. Significantly, Cheryl's newly purchased house was a mile from her daughter's home. Cheryl said she bought the house as an investment, but I feared she might decide to move to the Cape to help care for her young grandchildren. After she told me the details of her Thanksgiving visit and new purchase, I worried she would retire and leave Bethesda. That would end the possibility of our future together.

Amid my anxiety about our future, I started having dreams about Cheryl and awakened in the mornings to realize my feelings for her were more than friendship. A few days later, I risked sharing my dreams and flirtatiously said: "I'm interested and ready to take our friendship to the next step if you are." To my surprise, she coyly responded, "I'll have to think about that." I was shocked and confused, unsure if she was ambivalent about me or moving to the Cape. We spent December continuing our cautious dating, but we had numerous honest conversations about our friendship, our families, and our future, individually and as a couple. By January, we finally expressed our mutual desire to become sexually involved, and we were excited to see where "the next step" would take us in developing our new and deeper relationship.

The following year, we met each other's families and traveled together—to Rehoboth Beach and Lewes, Delaware, with friends; to Miami's South Beach and Key West, alone and just for fun. We became better friends with Julia and Carly, our first lesbian couple friends, and socialized with them often. Cheryl met my single adult children when they came home from Santa Cruz, California, and Philadelphia to visit me, and I went to Cape Cod to meet her daughter, daughter-in-law, and their two young children in Brewster. I also met her older daughter, who lived with her husband and three children in Concord, Massachusetts, near Boston.

⚜

In this first year, Cheryl and I began to see our personality differences more clearly, which allowed us to see how we could work out disagreements. Two months after we started dating romantically, we went to Rehoboth Beach for the weekend with a lesbian couple I knew. One woman was my neighbor, and she had started a new relationship about the same time I began dating Cheryl. The four of us shared a beach house for the weekend and enjoyed talking, getting to know each other, going out to dinner, and walking along the deserted boardwalk. It was early March and still off-season for the beach, so the area was not crowded. As we walked around the small beach town, our two friends held hands, so I reached out to hold Cheryl's hand. She pulled away and continued walking, acting like we were just friends, not girlfriends. I was confused, and I privately wondered and worried about what her refusal meant.

I wanted to be more "out" than Cheryl did and felt concerned she was experiencing internalized homophobia, which is not uncommon in the gay community among people who have not entirely accepted their sexuality. I had noticed similar anxiety in the behavior of a former girlfriend I dated between Linda and Cheryl, and I was certain I didn't want to enter another relationship with someone who felt uncomfortable with her sexuality. That night, Cheryl admitted she didn't feel comfortable with public displays of affection, but I remained concerned that her feelings were more than that. I wondered, would she have felt uncomfortable holding hands if she had been with a man? I realized this was our first conversation about who's right and who's wrong about being open in public, and I needed to discern if Cheryl was right for me.

We later talked about this incident several times. Eventually, we admitted that we both felt some anxiety about our new romantic relationship, but we handled our anxieties differently. I often jumped into things when nervous, ignoring my fears, while she tended to be cautious or hide. We had different methods of defending ourselves against issues that concerned us, even when we shared the same concerns. We sometimes projected our anxieties onto the other person. Understanding and communicating our differences and conflicts and expressing our underlying emotions with empathy became fundamental to our relationship's success, allowing us to find common ground, compromise, and avoid hurtful arguments.

After our Rehoboth weekend, I soon began attending St. Alban's and meeting more of Cheryl's church friends. She had a long-time connection to St. Alban's, which she had attended with John since their daughters were teens. Although I had a deep and meaningful history with St. Mark's, I felt it was part of my past life. I had stopped going to St. Mark's once I met Linda and later became absorbed in graduate school. I had changed too much over those years to feel like it was still my church home. The parishioners did not know the new me. In addition, St. Mark's was a Capitol Hill church and almost an hour from Cheryl's suburban home in Bethesda, so she was not interested in driving that far to church. Still idealizing my old community at St. Mark's, I struggled to fully settle into St. Alban's, yet I was eager to become part of Cheryl's community. At that point in our relationship, it mattered more to her that I attend her church than it mattered to me to return to St. Mark's.

After dating each other romantically for a year and a half, we decided to move in together. I rented out my Arlington home and moved into Cheryl's Bethesda home two years after we first met on our blind date in July 2001. By then, we knew each other's families, had shared our life histories and deepest secrets, and understood each other's strengths and weaknesses. We noticed our contrasting personality traits as well as our commonalities. We were comfortable with our differences and had learned how to communicate about them. After getting to know each other in-depth, we felt committed to each other as friends and life partners. By then, we knew we genuinely loved each other.

Our love was erotic, but it was distinct from the surprising infatuations we each encountered with our first girlfriends when we came out years earlier. It also differed from what we experienced with our husbands when we were younger and starting our families. Instead, our love felt solid and mature. It was grounded in vulnerable and intimate openness, a shared understanding of our long and evolving life journeys, and a comforting and enjoyable companionship. Our connection was rooted in a strong desire to be together for the rest of our lives.

On May 27, 2006, five years after we first met, Cheryl and I had a large commitment service and reception at St. Alban's, where we were then both members. Gay marriage was not yet legal in DC, but priests in the Episcopal Diocese of Washington were allowed to bless same-sex relationships. Our good friend, Julia, officiated our commitment service, which followed the words of the marital service in the Episcopal Book of Common Prayer. In addition to our friends and work colleagues, all our family members attended, including my two sisters and their husbands and our adult children and their spouses or partners. In the service, we were especially touched by a duet sung by Cheryl's daughter and daughter-in-law. The words of the old Shaker hymn they sang seemed to capture this moment of commitment in our lives:

> 'Tis the gift to be simple, 'tis the gift to be free,
> 'Tis the gift to come down where we ought to be,
> And when we find ourselves in the place just right,
> 'Twill be in the valley of love and delight.
> When true simplicity is gain'd,
> To bow and to bend we will not be ashamed,
> To turn, turn will be our delight,
> Till by turning, turning we come round right.[2]

Our marriage has been a joyful and fulfilling journey, filled with love and shared dreams—details I'll share more about in the next chapters. Eight years after our commitment service at St. Alban's, we began making plans to retire to Cape Cod. By then, the house Cheryl bought when we first met had become our future retirement home, and I was in love with the quaint town of Brewster as well as Cheryl. Filled with art galleries, antique stores, and a famous old country store with a pot-belly coal-burning stove, Brewster was named after William Brewster, the first religious leader of the Pilgrims. The town was renowned for its old sea captain's houses, many of which have become B&Bs. Our home was in the heart of Brewster, off the "Cranberry Highway" (Route 6A), and only a half-mile walk to Cape Cod Bay and one of Brewster's seven beaches. We planned to move the following year and decided to become legally married under Massachusetts law in preparation for our move. On July 20, 2014, we held a second small family wedding on Paine's Creek Beach near our home. Standing on the sand and facing Cape Cod Bay, Julia married us again.

Susanne, Julia, and Cheryl on Paine's Creek Beach

Cheryl and I have been together for 24 years. Our relationship is loving and strong, mainly because we can talk intimately and deeply with each other and generally feel understood. We still occasionally reminisce about what brought us together. We both believe one significant factor was our shared faith and acknowledge we could not have been with anyone seriously who was non-churched. Surprisingly to me, Cheryl was attracted to my life story of being raised in a religious home with a father who was a Southern Baptist minister. John was also raised in a religious family, and he, too, was a Baptist preacher's kid. She valued that in John, and it has mattered to her that he and I had that in common. She has said: "It was like adding icing on the cake when I found out you became Episcopalian after leaving the Baptist Church, just like John." It also mattered to her that St. Mark's had been so important in my young adult life, yet I was willing to join St. Alban's with her. Cheryl is most drawn to the liturgy and music of the Episcopal Church, and St. Alban's was well-known for that, while I am drawn to the sense of community and a place to belong, which once drew me to St. Mark's. These differences complement each other rather than compete. We can intensely discuss our spiritual beliefs, hopes and longings, questions and doubts, and sense of what feels Divine and Holy. We speak the same faith language, which is necessary for us both. Neither of us had this experience in our earlier relationships with women.

We also were drawn to each other because of our upbringing in the South and our family's backgrounds. We share a deep understanding and memory of what it was like to be raised in the Jim Crow South in white professional families, in an era of white supremacy, and in a world where People of Color experienced contemptible and vile discrimination. We remembered how our parents dealt with this culture and how we each felt some constraints about being a white girl or young woman in the South in the 1950s. In other words, we speak the same cultural language, and again, neither of us had this experience in any of our previous same-sex relationships.

Most importantly, we both had been married to men we loved, and our marriages ended sadly due to death or inevitable divorce. We had adult daughters who were gay, and we also transitioned sexually in middle age. No one we dated before meeting each other appreciated the process of going through these complex life experiences or this type of loss. We both saw how central these experiences have been to our lives and who we are today. We need to be with someone who understands these phenomena and who speaks the same relational and sexual language as we do. Neither of us had these unique experiences in our previous relationships.

Cheryl is not Linda, and they could not be more different. In hindsight, I remember experiencing Linda as charismatic, seductive, and the opposite of me, and now, the opposite of Cheryl. My chaotic and, at times, troubled relationship with Linda moved me from one stage of life to another, from one sexuality to another, at a time in my middle age when I was open to such a dramatic transition. I don't regret that my spontaneous relationship helped me transition sexually. Still, Linda was not the love of my life or aligned with my religious, cultural, and familial background and values.

On the other hand, Cheryl was and still is a fit for me. She is loving and calm, empathic and understanding, forgiving and spiritual. These characteristics matter to me more than all others at this stage in my life. I value her maturity, wisdom, steadiness, and loyalty. Most importantly, I value our intimacy and the love that binds us. As we move more deeply into our senior years, in our late 70s and 80s, I feel confident and grateful we will be with each other and care for each other for the remainder of our years.

For a New Beginning

By John O'Donohue

In out-of-the-way places of the heart,
Where your thoughts never think to wander,
This beginning has been quietly forming,
Waiting until you were ready to emerge.

For a long time it has watched your desire,
Feeling the emptiness growing inside you,
Noticing how you willed yourself on,
Still unable to leave what you had outgrown.

It watched you play with the seduction of safety
And the gray promises that sameness whispered,
Heard the waves of turmoil rise and relent,
Wondered would you always live like this.

Then the delight, when your courage kindled,
And out you stepped onto new ground,
Your eyes young again with energy and dream,
A path of plenitude opening before you.

—O'Donohue, J. (2008). *To bless the space between us: A book of blessings.*
New York: Penguin Random House, p. 14.

Nine

Vocational Commitment

May the work fit the rhythms of your soul,
Enabling you to draw from the invisible
New ideas and a vision that will inspire.

—*John O'Donohue*[1]

In the second year of our relationship, Cheryl played an essential role in helping me secure a faculty position at the National Catholic School of Social Service (NCSSS), which is part of The Catholic University of America (CUA) in Northeast DC. I was practicing full-time as a psychotherapist but had been searching for an academic position to use my doctoral education more expansively. When I graduated from Smith, my main goal was to obtain a full-time academic position in a social work school to give back to the next generation of professionals. To be honest, I also wanted a university position for its retirement benefits. In addition to being a therapist in private practice, Cheryl was teaching at NCSSS as an adjunct social work instructor and doing training for the foreign service, drawing on her years of living in other countries. She introduced me to an NCSSS faculty friend, who encouraged me to apply for a tenure-line faculty position that had just become available.

Surprisingly, my sexual identity did not prevent me from being hired at this prominent Catholic institution, and I accepted a position as a tenure-line full-time Assistant Professor at NCSSS two months after I began living with Cheryl. As an academic, I hoped to continue my dissertation research on lesbian families and wanted to compare lesbian and gay male families with children. This was a plan I discussed with the faculty when I applied for the position. Soon after I joined the faculty, however, my Dean called me into his office. He said, "Susanne, you need to know that you probably won't get tenure if you continue to conduct research and write about gay individuals or families." I was stunned. "This was not the impression I received when the faculty interviewed me, and you hired me for this job," I said. "In fact, you all seemed really interested in my work and wanted me to do more of it." He acknowledged that was true but told me the CUA Provost had been conversing with him about me. To my surprise, the Provost had read all my publications, including my dissertation, to assure himself I was not writing anything that disagreed with Catholic doctrine.

It became clear I was fighting a losing battle regarding my academic dreams. I could continue with my plans to focus on gay families and risk not getting tenure, or I could refocus my professional scholarship and increase my tenure odds. I was disappointed and frustrated, but I respected my dean's assessment of the Provost's concerns. I knew what I had to do professionally, given my age. I was too old to begin searching for another tenure-line faculty position at another university, which would likely be out of town. And it was unlikely I would find one. I decided to try to make the best of this unexpected situation.

Instead of continuing my research on gay families, I shifted my focus to attachment theory itself since it had been the theoretical foundation of my dissertation. As I delved further into the vast amount of research on attachment, I became familiar with a newly created evidence-based intervention program for parents and young children called Circle of Security®,[2] based on Mary Ainsworth's research about early child development. After my dissertation, I had been keeping up with the latest attachment research, and the Circle of Security® program[3] caught my attention. The program trains parents to respond to their children in a manner that increases the child's sense of security with the parent. When I read about this program, I was impressed with its outcomes. Although I decided not to personally become a trainer, I did refer one of my private clients to the program for their child. I also used the program's concepts for my research at NCSSS. The Circle of Security® program has now gained international acclaim.[4]

The concept of the *circle of security* is based on Ainsworth's observations that when young toddlers feel secure, they move away from their secure base to explore the world beyond their attachment figure. Once they move away, they eventually stumble and fall and then return to their attachment figure's safe haven to seek reassurance and security again. This circular process reminds me of my toddlers learning to walk. I would hold their hands as they gingerly tiptoed along. Eventually, they felt secure and let go of my hand to head out across the room until they fell, quickly turned around, and came crawling back to the safety of my waiting arms. In contrast, if young children have an anxious attachment, rather than secure, they are afraid to explore beyond the safety of their home base. Or, if their attachment is avoidant, they are reluctant to return for help after they explore and fall.

Feeling secure, exploring, stumbling, and returning to one's safe haven is a secure circular process that continues throughout human development. The process occurs when children leave their secure base to explore their physical abilities, develop cognitive skills, and navigate new relationships and emotional dynamics. They return to their safe haven for reassurance and support to regain their sense of security. Attachment relationships change as we age, but the circular dynamic process of returning to a safe haven when needed is life-long. As a teen, I experienced the circle of security phenomenon when I felt secure enough with my father to challenge his religious beliefs before I went to college—to explore beyond his teachings. Yet, when I struggled academically in my freshman year, he was the first person I called for reassurance and support. I still engage in this circular process when I share my concerns, doubts, and inner thoughts with Cheryl, my current primary attachment figure. I seek her loving support, comfort, and wise perspective as my safe haven when needed.

As a professor, I started applying attachment theory and research to understand the dynamics in adult relationships, such as supervisor-supervisee, clinician-client, teacher-student, and adult child-elder-parent relationships. I also applied the circle of security process to relationships beyond the parent-child relationship. The first article I wrote after joining the faculty used the concept of the circle of security to conceptualize supervisory relationships between social work graduate students and their fieldwork supervisors. I offered suggestions about how the supervisor could provide a secure base for the student, thus increasing the student's confidence and professional development. By my second year at NCSSS, I created an ongoing popular course, *Attachment Theory and Neurobiology*. In addition, a colleague and I combined our compatible ideas and wrote numerous articles on social work field education and supervision. We created a supervision training program based on the circle of security concepts and then tested and published our program's effectiveness. Eventually, I co-edited a textbook on *Adult Attachment in Clinical Social Work*.[5] My clinical practice, teaching experience, and research enabled me to see how attachment patterns and processes are central to all human relationships. I also became convinced that the circular dynamic process of returning to a safe haven when needed is a life-long phenomenon.

The highlight of my academic career was teaching Human Behavior and the Social Environment in a social work program on the war-torn island of Mindanao, the southernmost island of the Philippines.[6] This peace-building program was called the Social Work Education Project (SWEP) and was co-created by a senior NCSSS faculty member and former Dean, Dr. Fred Ahearn, and a former NCSSS graduate who lived in the Philippines, Dr. Steve Muncy. I immediately wanted to participate in SWEP because I had never traveled to a developing country. The opportunity evoked memories of my adolescent desire to join the Peace Corps and my 10-year-old dream of becoming a missionary. The primary goal of SWEP was to educate bachelor's level social workers to obtain a Masters in Teaching Social Work degree from Catholic University to serve as leaders and teachers in the conflict-affected areas of Mindanao. The majority of our 100 Filipino students were Muslim, though a few were Christian, and many had been internally displaced due to the long-term violent conflicts in their country.

During my six weeks in the Philippines, spread out over two years, I became close friends with Steve and with his young Filipino assistant, Joseph. American-born and raised, Steve lived his adult life in the Philippines, where he created Community and Family Services International (CFSI),[7] a Manila-based humanitarian NGO that served the Philippines and Vietnam. Steve was mentoring Joseph in leadership for his organization. A thoughtful young man in his late 20s, Joseph was exceptionally intelligent and a college graduate. He was born and raised in a loving but impoverished family in Manilla, where he still lived with his parents and adult siblings. Joseph became my cultural guide in all the weeks I was in the Philippines, and we spent many hours sharing our life experiences and impressions of our respective cultures.

When Steve, Joseph, and I flew the 700 miles from Manilla to Cotabato City in Mindanao to begin my first week of teaching in the SWEP program, Joseph and I were both excited but anxious. I had not traveled outside the U.S. other than my Christmas week with my children in Paris many years earlier, and though Filipino, Joseph had never traveled to Mindanao. The island had a warranted reputation for being dangerous and was on the U.S. State Department's "do not travel" list, in part due to the kidnapping of Westerners. When we approached Cotabato City, I looked out the plane window and could see coconut palms waving in ponds of water near the airport. As the tension grew inside me, I put on my hijab to cover my blond hair, in order to be sensitive to the local culture. Once we landed, I quickly walked down the plane's ramp. I saw dozens of armed military guards surrounding the entrance of the small airport and dozens more Filipino faces staring intently at me inside the terminal. For the next week, I saw no other white person, except for Steve.

During my first trip to Cotabato City, I experienced the shock, anxiety, and sometimes fear of being in a totally foreign culture. I was there without anyone from the U.S., and I was a white person in a war-torn, still developing country. I was intimidated by the heavy military presence of young men walking around town with rifles slung over their shoulders and the outbursts of violence that occurred on the street while I was teaching. I was astounded by the overwhelming poverty unlike any I had witnessed, far worse than the poverty of downtown Louisville or other urban or rural areas in the U.S. I found myself appalled and saddened by the sexist ways women were treated in response to sexual abuse and rape. In class discussions about families, politics, and religious life in Mindanao, I learned about the long, complex history of war in the Philippines and how the United States had contributed to the country's many problems.

In contrast to aspects of Filipino culture that I found upsetting, I was fascinated by the meals, dress, and religious norms. I was amazed that my Muslim female students wore hijabs outside of class but removed them while in the classroom, and I was told this was a sign of how comfortable and safe they felt. I was envious of my students' warm and caring social connections, which differed from the Western individualism and competition I witnessed among my American students. These Filipinos were open and loving to each other and me. My students expressed much curiosity about the details of my American life; I shared that I was a mother of two adult children and a grandmother, a social work clinician, and a professor. Yet, I was careful not to reveal my sexual identity or my political and religious beliefs because I assumed my students would not understand or approve. I aimed to appreciate and respect their culture and not create a barrier to their learning by emphasizing my cultural differences. I was there to be of service and to teach, not to reveal my personal story, and I understood that all of my identity didn't need to be highlighted in order to do this work.

There were innumerable moments in this teaching experience when I became suddenly aware and deeply moved by these cultural differences. One day, I was teaching about chaos theory, a human behavior theory social workers use to describe unpredictable changes that occur seemingly randomly because of small events. This phenomenon and the effect of random change is sometimes called the *butterfly effect*. I was concerned that my students might struggle to grasp this abstract theory or understand the Southern accent of my English. Although Filipinos learn English in school, their primary language is Tagalog, and I had become aware some students were not as proficient in English as others. As I tried to explain the theory, I suddenly noticed one of my students, a quiet and small young woman who rarely spoke in English or in class, had started crying. Confused and concerned, I stopped the class to learn what was happening. Everyone quickly started talking in Tagalog, and several more began to cry. With the help of an older student who served as my interpreter, I learned the younger woman understood everything I was saying in English. Her tears came because my words triggered memories of losing her home and family members due to the random effects of war in her country. I listened with shock, sadness, and empathy while all the students in my class began to share about the chaos they knew all too well, teaching me the rest of the hour about their culture and war.

I often had long conversations with Joseph, who was non-religious, about his life and the lives of our students, frequently talking with him about the extreme poverty we saw around us. He knew the truth about my sexuality and my religious background, and he shared with me about his own life and upbringing. He said to me one day, "You know, Susanne, it's all about luck. I am who I am, and you are who you are based on pure luck. It's all luck where you were born and into what culture you were raised. Luck shapes who we all are." His astute observation made sense to me. I could imagine how successful Joseph would be by Western standards if he had been born and educated in a socio-economically stable American family. I remembered lying in the bed of four-leaf clovers behind my Red Springs church when I was a young child, wondering about luck and its meaning in my life. I now realized I was right as a child–I was quite lucky to grow up where I did with a supportive, stable family. And that luck had led me here.

Throughout my three long trips to the Philippines, my involvement with SWEP was personally and professionally enriching. I became acutely aware of my white, Western privilege—my "luck"—and how I felt being a racial and religious minority in a developing country amid war and displacement. I also became aware of the prevalent kidnapping of Westerners in Mindanao and how that posed as a bad luck risk for me. Yet, through all these experiences, I discovered how to bridge cultural differences with my students and Joseph through mutual openness and empathy. I am forever grateful for this life-shaping experience.

❦

In addition to my positive teaching experiences at NCSSS, it is also essential to underscore the Catholic affiliation of this social work school—and how that affected me during my 12 years on the faculty. Faculty members were encouraged to incorporate the study of spirituality into the curriculum. This expectation was comfortable because it aligned with social work's theory that bio-psycho-social-spiritual factors shape human development and behavior. However, I was made immediately aware of how university administrators were unsupportive of scholarship on gays and lesbians due to Catholic religious doctrines about sexuality, especially the church's critical views about gay marriage. I was a non-Catholic, openly gay faculty member in a same-sex marriage. When I was hired, I was the only full-time social work faculty member who was not Catholic by religion or a graduate with a social work degree from CUA. I was an outsider, and I felt it.

Before I received tenure, I occasionally worried the administration might try to fire me when I saw a few other conservative Catholic schools around the country firing their gay employees. Although I usually found acceptance and appreciation from my colleagues in the social work school, the university administration's increasing alignment with the conservative Roman Catholic Church made me feel excluded. In the end, reorienting the focus of my research to attachment theory was a positive and productive decision. As a result of my research and publications, I was granted tenure and promotion in 2009. I later heard this was a surprise to some faculty members, who voted for me but feared the University trustees would not accept me because I was gay.

Once I received tenure, I returned to my initial interests and published on clinical practice with lesbian, gay, and bisexual individuals.[8] I also became more open about myself, my sexuality, and my gay marriage, realizing that silence about my identity and family had taken an emotional toll on me. It had been a "toxic silence,"[9] to use Cassidy Hall's words, maintained solely to gain tenure. My newly acquired tenure gave me a blanket of safety, but I still found it challenging to be authentic in the face of Catholic dogma. Although I had been promoted to Associate Professor, I knew I would never become a full professor without active involvement in the larger university. I struggled to find a way to make that happen.

After I returned from the Philippines and received tenure, CUA selected a new Provost for the university and a new Dean for the social work school. All the CUA administrators at that time were more conservative than their predecessors who hired me, and they appeared more committed to promoting Catholic doctrines. After the new Dean came, he ignored me for committee appointments, and I was omitted from work groups. Some of my colleagues noticed and expressed surprise, seeing that I was being frozen out of opportunities for further advancement.

One day, the new Dean selected members for a committee he formed that I should have chaired, given my interests and skills, yet I was not even chosen as a member. I left my office in tears and walked to another part of the campus to cry. A close colleague came running after me to offer her consolation. We agreed that he seemed to want me to leave NCSSS and that it was likely because I was gay. Except for a few sympathetic faculty friends, I felt utterly alone and thought I must return to the toxic silence I had maintained before my tenure.

I was not the only one feeling the administration's lack of support for LGBTQIA+ research and scholarship. One day, a large number of students gathered on the campus lawn to protest an administration action related to gay issues. I hesitated to participate, not wanting to antagonize the administration further, but at the last moment, I decided to join the group to show my support. As we all held hands and sang, a student standing beside me—someone I had never taught and did not know—silently placed a round button into my hand.

This small but powerful gesture brought me to tears because I felt she was telling me in an unspoken message that she knew about my identity and that she, along with God, accepted me. I promised myself that when I retired, I would continue advocating for and supporting the LGBTQIA+ community.

The experience of being on the margins of CUA due to my sexuality deepened my faith and further strengthened my views about my sexuality. It also prompted me to retire at age 68. I might have worked a few more years if I had felt less shunned by the Dean and administration. However, as I approached retirement from full-time employment, both my faith and my sexuality transitioned into the stage that McLaren describes as "harmony," where the dualism of simplicity, the pragmatism of complexity, and the suspicion of perplexity finally give way to love. Importantly, all the previous stages of faith are vital to this last stage. As McLaren says, "Doubt prepares the way for a new kind of faith after (and with) doubt, a humbled and harmonious faith, a faith that expresses itself in love."[10]

Teaching at a university where my faith and sexuality were marginalized was the crisis and challenge that finally pushed me into this fourth phase of development. I realized the administration would never accept me at CUA, and acceptance there no longer mattered. I let it go because I didn't need the CUA administration's approval to feel comfortable with my career or my life. I felt "God loves me just as I am."

Despite my feelings of being marginalized at times, my years at NCSSS were some of the most rewarding of my social work career. I enjoyed teaching and interacting with social work graduate students and mentoring doctoral students on their dissertations; my work with my students was deeply meaningful to me and to them. I enjoyed conducting research, writing academic papers and books, and exploring theories and new ideas; my scholarly work was well-regarded both locally and in the national social work community. I also developed life-changing relationships with students and colleagues in the Philippines and built warm professional and personal relationships with my NCSSS friends; I knew these relationships would continue after I retired.

Importantly, during these twelve years, my relationship with my wife was loving and solid, deepening the longer we lived together. A few years into my tenure at NCSSS, Cheryl retired from teaching as an adjunct, but she knew the faculty, understood the university politics, and remained my safe haven at the end of the day when I would share with her the hurt I sometimes felt and my growing frustration with the CUA administration. She fully supported my decision to retire from full-time employment when I did. I realized I was ready, and it was time to move on. Cheryl was still practicing as a psychotherapist, but she also was ready to retire. We felt grateful that we could both retire simultaneously and move together to a different community at this time in our lives.

As we prepared to move to our home on Cape Cod, we joined a retirement support group at St. Alban's. For half a year, we shared our uncertainties and hopes with a small group of parishioners who also planned to retire within the year. This group, plus our ongoing conversations with each other, built our confidence that we were making the right decision for this stage in our lives. As we talked with each other, I realized I was pleased about my life's direction and grateful I had navigated the tensions and transitions of middle age. I felt indebted to my parents for leaving me the financial means to obtain my doctorate and move into academia. I felt blessed that Cheryl introduced me to NCSSS, enabling me to receive my faculty position.

I also felt deep gratitude to the Holy Spirit that sustained me through the highs and lows of my twelve years of full-time academic life. The grace of God made it possible for me to obtain this job, and now I felt God calling me to leave. McLaren says that harmony is a phase in life when "a new music begins, faintly at first but rising to a steady crescendo, a music of appreciation, empathy, wonder, and, yes, all-embracing love."[11] As I approached this final phase of life, I could hear the sound of new music. I hoped retirement would bring adventure and discovery. I looked forward to establishing a new home with Cheryl, creating fresh life rhythms and activities, building a different community of friends, and relaxing after 43 years of full-time employment.

For Retirement

By John O'Donohue

This is where your life has arrived,
After all the years of effort and toil;
Look back with graciousness and thanks
On all your great and quiet achievements

Now is the time to enjoy your heart's desire,
To live the dreams you've waited for,
To awaken the depths beyond your work
And enter into your infinite source.

—O'Donohue, J. (2008). *To bless the space between us: A book of blessings.* New York: Penguin Random House, p. 167.

Part Four

Late Adulthood

Ten

Retirement Harmony

You stand on the shore of new invitation
To open your life to what is left undone.

—*John O'Donohue*[1]

Beginning our new chapter of retirement, Cheryl and I settled into our surroundings on Cape Cod during the week of Christmas 2015. We renovated our Brewster home over the next few years, joined St. Mary's Episcopal Church in Barnstable Village, and developed several new friends, all "wash-ashore" retirees like us. I facilitated some church groups at St. Mary's and joined others, especially groups focused on faith and racism. I led support groups at a nearby senior center, including groups for LGBTQIA+ seniors. I taught as a part-time adjunct professor and online research advisor at Smith College, my alma mater. And I spent my second year driving to Boston to provide part-time childcare for my daughter's newborn baby. My retirement was unfolding the way I had hoped it would.

Cheryl and I also took trips within the U.S. and abroad, including travels to National Parks, a week in London, and two river cruises with Julia and Carly through Europe. We participated in a meaningful, week-long contemplative retreat on the island of Iona, Scotland, with a group from our church. Although I enjoyed these retreats and vacations, I remembered Joseph's observation of how lucky I was. Part of me relished the privilege of participating in these vacations, and another part felt drawn to serve others more than centering on my pleasure. Then

COVID-19 hit the world, and everything seemed to change and come into sharper focus.

Fear of death moved to the forefront of my mind as people in my immediate community and across the world became infected with this virus, and millions of people died. Going into lockdown and wearing masks whenever I ventured outside to buy necessities changed the newly developed rhythm of my life. Denial no longer worked as a defense mechanism against the virus touching us. Cheryl and I lost contact with most of our new Cape Cod acquaintances. We had to connect with relatives on Zoom and felt concerned about them becoming ill or losing their jobs, as COVID upended all aspects of life. We eagerly awaited the promised COVID-19 vaccine. These life changes triggered by COVID made me focus on who and what I most valued in life, and they also served to shake my faith.

⚜

As COVID began to sweep across the country in March 2020, I would sit alone in the mornings beside the large picture window in my living room, staring out at the bare trees of the woods in front of my home. The cold, grey, windy Cape weather showed no signs of spring and matched my mood. I was tearful, aware of my growing fear about the events unfolding in Boston and New York hospitals. I had visited my son and granddaughter in sunny Los Angeles only a few weeks earlier. The world there was beautiful and predictable, but now, back on the East Coast, news reports suggested the world had turned upside-down. As reports about the impact of COVID monopolized the news cycle, our state moved into lockdown. All local activities were canceled.

Looking outside at the desolate winter landscape, I wondered where God was during this unpredictable world pandemic. I did not believe in a higher power pulling the strings of the universe like a controlling puppeteer, but still, I was flooded with my adolescent doubts about the existence of God. Memories about the despair I had felt during the early stages of my divorce years ago came rushing back, and my current anxiety felt similar. As a professional, I knew how significant loss could trigger memories of earlier losses in life, and I felt that process unfolding within me. I felt shaken physically, emotionally, and spiritually. The harmony I had been experiencing in my faith before retirement evaporated back into perplexity, that phase filled with doubts, of seeing God as a myth, of being in a dark tunnel of unknowing. I struggled with a foggy sense of doubt about the mystery of God and a world that was becoming overwhelmed with death.

After St. Mary's canceled all in-person meetings, Cheryl and I started meeting on Zoom with a small group of women friends from church. During a discussion of the Lenten study book we were reading, Ta-Nehisi Coates' *The Water Dancer*,[2] we talked about coping with our fears as older women at high risk for catching COVID. My friends shared how praying and feeling God's presence helped them, but I was in further despair. Prayer seemed confusing and ineffective for me. I was unable to find spiritual relief because I had returned to feelings of doubt and grief that were all too familiar from past years.

In both desperation and hope, I sought out spiritual direction to help me with my confusion more privately and profoundly. I felt this would be more beneficial for me than additional psychotherapy because my anxiety was related to my spirituality. My long-time close friend, Julia, referred me to my first spiritual director. I cried throughout my initial conversation with Jacques as I shared the history of my faith and my sexuality. An Episcopal priest from the DC metro area, Jacques was familiar with St. Mark's and understood the religious transformation I experienced in that faith community after my divorce. He also appreciated the power of my early religious education and expressed empathy for my current confusion. I spoke with him by phone weekly, then biweekly for almost a year until I moved to several more years of monthly conversations. His guidance grounded and supported me as I pieced together the jigsaw puzzle of my life.

Around the time I began working with Jacques, George Floyd was killed, adding to the country's upheaval in the early months of the COVID pandemic. I was horrified watching the television coverage of his murder, played over and over, and I was moved by the wave of protests throughout the nation in response. A Smith doctoral student I mentored on Zoom—a middle-aged Black woman in Los Angeles—told me she was pleased but "surprised to see so many white folks out there protesting with us." I began to see the considerable significance of Floyd's murder, igniting a wake-up call to white Americans to see how racist this country continues to be. I was reminded of the racism I witnessed as a child in the Jim Crow South, where there was enforced segregation and an active and violent KKK. I saw clearly that not enough has changed over the years.

Our St. Mary's priest also noticed the anti-racist responses exploding around the country and felt called to help our predominantly white parish become better attuned to issues of race and racism. She wanted the congregation to participate in a newly created national Episcopal Church program called Sacred Ground,[3] a film-based dialogue series focused on race, racism, and faith. The year before COVID, Cheryl and I joined six other parishioners to complete Sacred Ground as a pilot program, and we eagerly volunteered to lead it for the whole parish. Yet, we were shocked when over 100 people registered for the 10-week program and realized that accommodating so many people would require additional facilitators. The flood of interest seemed linked with distress about George Floyd's murder and a desire to talk about race, plus people were hungry to see each other, even virtually, amid COVID.

After much conversation and planning, we organized ten Zoom groups with two co-facilitators per group. Cheryl and I each led two of the groups, but we didn't co-facilitate with each other. Over five months, the Zoom groups met every other week for two hours to dialogue about the assigned content. The online curriculum included readings and intense, provocative videos that provided a deep dive into the history of racism among European Americans and Indigenous people, African Americans, Latin Americans, and Asian Americans. The material also focused on the effects of white supremacy, both past and present, and how our faith calls us to respond to racism.

One of our required Sacred Ground texts was *Jesus and the Disinherited* by Howard Thurman,[4] who inspired Martin Luther King, Jr., during the civil rights movement. Thurman was not an activist, but instead a Black minister, theologian, and Christian mystic. He served as an older spiritual mentor to Dr. King, influencing his views on nonviolence. Reportedly, Dr. King always kept a well-read copy of *Jesus and the Disinherited* in his pocket and often quoted Thurman in his sermons and addresses during his protests.

I served as one of two co-administrators of our Sacred Ground program. I used my academic skills in curriculum planning to create outlines for all the groups to follow so there would be some uniformity. I met every other week for a couple of hours online with David, my co-administrator, as we talked in depth about the Sacred Ground content, reviewed the videos, and intimately shared our feelings about racism and how this content stirred us. We then each led our two groups for others in the parish, rewatching the videos in preparation. Sharing with David was a profound, revealing, and intimate process that I deeply valued. However, meeting with him and then facilitating two more Sacred Ground groups with my assigned parishioners was quite intense and draining.

When our Sacred Ground program concluded, I was exhausted but felt transformed by the process. The content was ground-shaking, prompting my reflection about my childhood experiences in the 1950s South that I had not fully understood or processed. I realized how privileged and over-protected I was because of my race, the way I was raised, and the respect my family had in our community. Although Dad supported civil rights and was educated as a minister and social worker, plus my parents were both genuinely concerned about marginalized people in the world, there was much they did not know and could not teach me. I doubt they knew of the horrors we learned in the Sacred Ground program because this history was not taught in my schools and definitely not in theirs. In all my years of graduate social work education, I also had not learned the extent of racist hate that was exposed in the Sacred Ground program.

Sacred Ground left me wiser and deeply sorrowful. I wondered if my English ancestors, who came to this country in the late 1700s and settled in the mountains of North Carolina, were complicit in the displacement of the Cherokee Indians out of Appalachia. I regretted I had not focused more as a professional social worker on social justice issues, working instead with relatively privileged white adults doing psychotherapy and teaching. I wish I had used my social work skills to do more to address systemic and structural racism.[5] The emotions I experienced in Sacred Ground were intense, and I'm grateful for the experience of increasing my understanding of America's history with race and owning my role in it.

The Sacred Ground program also deepened my spiritual life. I became more attuned to the power of contemplation and Jesus' radical message of love for people on the margins of society. I became familiar with Thurman's profound writings and why he says Jesus' teachings have something to say "to those who stand at a moment in human history with their backs against the wall...the poor, the disinherited, the dispossessed."[6] I came to understand the place of grief in my own spiritual life and the healing power of shared communal sorrow as I faced my hurts and owned how I had hurt others.

I've now facilitated or participated in the Sacred Ground program five times, and every time I re-watch the videos and re-read the assignments, I am repulsed by the history. When I watched the same films from one year of Sacred Ground to the next, I realized I did not always remember what I had previously seen. The historical events and stories presented in these videos were so disturbing and traumatic that I blocked out the horrific events I saw. This phenomenon made me realize that as a white person, I unconsciously was obscuring racism's horrors due to my privilege of *not* being on the margins of society due to race.

At the same time, I realized I *am* on the margins of society because of my age, my gender, and my sexual orientation. Although I'm white and well-educated, I often feel like a misfit in a country that values and prefers youth and beauty, wealth and success, the male gender and heterosexuality, and heterosexual marriage. Being where I am at this stage of life, I sometimes wonder how I can contribute to society and what my purpose in life is now. I wonder how or if I can still make a difference in people's lives and how I can address the issues of inequality, racism, sexism, and homophobia. As I ponder these questions, I'm reminded of the words of Forrest Cuch of the Ute Tribe, who speaks about his people in the Sacred Ground film "Native Voices: Speaking to the Church and the World." He says:

> *If we look deeply within our soul to find out who we are,*
> *we can make deep contributions to this world.*[7]

⁂

I resonate with Cuch's words and feel called to look more deeply within my soul and my true self. A year after I started spiritual direction and Sacred Ground, I began the Living School. This two-year spiritual formation program is part of the Center for Action and Contemplation in Albuquerque, New Mexico.[8] Founded by Fr. Richard Rohr, a Franciscan Catholic priest, the Living School fulfilled my desire to look more deeply within my soul for a greater understanding of contemplation, spirituality, and compassionate engagement with people on society's margins. Despite the challenges posed by the early years of the pandemic, this hybrid online and in-person program met my spiritual needs by providing me with opportunities to form authentic friendships with like-minded individuals who were on similar spiritual journeys and had similar questions.

The last in-person week of my Living School program in July 2023 was personally consequential. The week focused on the future of engaged contemplation and how to apply the wisdom we learned during the previous two years of the program. Brian McLaren, now the Dean of the Living School, stressed that we needed to engage with a world filled with discord, hatred, and violence regarding diversity, or, as he said, "a world on fire." Tears welled in my eyes as he talked because I felt pulled to engage with a world on fire about diversity. In this final symposium, I told the whole group I felt on fire. I'm living in a world that seems to hate my family members because some of them identify as nonbinary or trans. In the years after COVID began, Cheryl and I learned that three of our eight grandchildren identify as nonbinary or trans. Two of hers are now post-college, and my grandchild is in elementary school. I was feeling a growing concern about the safety and the future of our grandchildren.

After the symposium, half a dozen participants came to me to thank me for what I said because they were having similar experiences. This felt like a sign that there's a need for family members of trans or nonbinary children to talk with a spiritual companion who understands these issues, speaks their language, and recognizes there is no single right way to express or experience sexuality and gender. In that last Living School symposium, I felt drawn to work as a spiritual director or companion with those who feel themselves on society's margins for whatever reason.

I am especially drawn to serve as a spiritual advisor/companion working with the LGBTQIA+ community and with families of sexually non-conforming people. My personal and professional experience has attuned me to the stigma, hatred, and homophobia that LGBTQIA+ people experience. Shortly after my Living School program ended, I applied to Stillpoint, a Los Angeles-based spiritual formation program focused on "the art of spiritual direction."[9] I currently participate in Stillpoint's online program, training to be a spiritual companion with a special focus on trans and nonbinary individuals and their families, as well as the broader LGBTQIA+ community.

In the late decades of the 20th century, when Robert came out, it was challenging and, at times, unsafe and frightening to be openly gay. Now, in the 21st century, trans or nonbinary people are faced with the stigma, hatred, and phobia that gay people felt 50 or more years ago. I'm troubled by this hatred in general, but I feel saddened and worried for members of my own diverse family. As a professional social worker, I worry about what the future holds for our trans and nonbinary grandchildren as they navigate differences and stigma in the current American culture filled with intolerance and hate. As an older woman in my last phase of life, I wonder why three young people in our family identify as nonbinary or trans at this time in history and how this came to be. And as a grandmother, I feel a deep love for all our grandchildren, especially these three. I hope they will continue to be excited by life, appreciate their creativity and gifts, and remain determined to be true to themselves. I also pray that they always feel accepted and blessed by the unconditional love they receive from me, Cheryl, and our extended families.

The experience of having nonbinary grandchildren does not shake my faith. Instead, it reminds me that sexuality and faith share a common feature in terms of their fluidity. My life experiences suggest that sexuality and gender, and spirituality and faith, are dynamic, nonbinary processes. Sexuality and gender may change over a person's lifetime, just as one's faith and spirituality may evolve. Looking at sexual orientation and gender in a nonbinary, nondual manner suggests there is no single right way to express or experience sexuality and gender. Likewise, viewing faith through a more inclusive lens recognizes many ways to experience the Divine and what is Holy, not just one way. There's a need to help sexually non-conforming individuals and their families accept that "God loves me just as I am."

Now that I'm in my late adulthood and have completed Sacred Ground and the Living School, I have fully moved into the last phase of faith McLaren calls "harmony."[10] I've moved beyond the fears I felt at the beginning of COVID, which perplexed and returned me to a place of unknowing about God's presence. I've become more aware of the power of love, contemplation, and shared community to act against hatred and fear of difference and people on life's margins. In this harmony phase of faith, I perceive God's presence in my loving relationships, life experiences, and commitment to inclusion, knowing we are all connected. Similarly, as my marriage to Cheryl has deepened and we face the last stage of our lives together, I feel the presence of harmony in my sexuality. I am grateful we found each other and feel united in our love and hope for the future through our intimacy. Doubt is no longer a threat to my faith or my sexuality but an understandable and predictable part of it.

In this last phase of life, I see my faith and my sexuality as nondual processes, as suggested in the words of McLaren:

> We encounter the love of God in others. Most obviously, we do so in moments of intimacy and kindness, when God flows like an alternating current among us. But we also encounter divine love in times of conflict, as our hearts break, as we feel wound and absence, and as we weep and work for reconciliation and peace. Beyond intimacy and conflict among those closest to us, we humans encounter and experience divine love in the experience of the other, the stranger, the outsider, the outcast, and even the enemy.[11]

These words capture my understanding of nonduality, of God flowing "like an alternating current." Love exists in both intimacy and conflict, in both kindness and woundedness. Divine love is within us, within the outsider, and even within the enemy.

As I embrace this final stage of faith, it has been five years since the first signs of COVID rocked the world and ten years since I retired. Time has indeed flown or somehow disappeared, and I am undeniably in old age. My close friends and I joke or complain about growing old, and then we all acknowledge we have arrived. Many of us are now living with age-related illnesses, some chronic, some acute, reminding us of the perils of aging. Cheryl and I are both in reasonably good health for women in our late 70s and 80s, but we're more conscious of the 10-year age gap between us than when we first met. The difference in our ages leaves me contemplating: "Will I outlive her? How will I manage, and what will I do in my remaining years?"

Although I can't know the future, what I do know is that my faith and my sexuality are both finally in a stage of harmony at this phase of my life. I have gone through the questions and doubts of early life, the love and loss of a first marriage, followed by despair and loneliness after divorce. In middle age, I went through the surprise, confusion, and joy that came through exploring and transitioning my sexuality. Since age 50, I've significantly grown professionally and personally due to my education, second marriage, and academic career. Since retirement, I've negotiated the return of my doubts evoked by COVID, engaged in spiritual direction, and moved into an exploration of both racism and spiritual contemplation.

Now I'm deeply involved in formation as a spiritual companion with others while I continue on my own spiritual path. As McLaren says, "the processes, struggles, experiences, practices, and intervening stages" are necessary to make "harmony go from impossible to fleeting to hard to habitual to normative."[12] From the perspective of old age wisdom, I could not be who or where I am today without having gone through where I've been and without having the sense of God's companionship along the way.

From Psalms

God is our refuge and our strength,
A very present help in trouble.
Therefore we will not fear, though the earth be moved,
And though the mountains be toppled into
The depths of the sea.

—Psalm 46:1-2, RSV

Lord, you have searched me out and known me;
You know my sitting down and my rising up;
You discern my thoughts from afar.
You trace my journeys and my resting place
and are acquainted with all my ways.

—Psalm 139:1-2, RSV

Epilogue

My True Self

The first half of life is discovering the script,
and the second half is actually writing it and owning it.

—*Richard Rohr*[1]

I now know that reminiscing and sharing my stories helped me see the bigger picture and empowered me to write and own the script for my life. This has clarified for me the two foundational themes of my *evolving faith* and *fluid sexuality*. The more I contemplate these themes, the more I see the intersection between them—like the two roads meeting at the intersection of my early childhood home. Both my faith and sexuality are dynamic processes, winding roads that, after crisscrossing over the years, have come together at a point of alignment at this time in my life. They converge with one central question: "What is my authentic true self?" Considering my development and the changes in both my faith and sexuality, I wonder: "Was I once living a false self, or have I always lived my true self?" As I ponder my relationships based on my early childhood, I also wonder: "How have my attachments shaped the development of my sexuality, my faith, and my true self?"

Upon reflection, I have come to see that my evolving faith and fluid sexuality are related to being true to myself. As my religious beliefs developed, I initially hesitated to share my true self with my parents out of respect and concern for their reactions. However, by the time I entered young adulthood, I felt at ease in revealing my true self regarding my faith. During middle age, as my sexuality transitioned, my actions reflected my developing true self, and I was comfortable revealing my sexuality to my family and friends. Instead of transitioning from a false-self sexuality in early adulthood to a true-self sexuality later in life, my experience illustrates the fluid and flexible nature of sexuality and gender, which can occur at any point during development. As I see it, the religious beliefs I held in early childhood and my sexuality in young adulthood were both authentic aspects of my true self during those stages of development. Feeling love and acceptance from others early in life gave me the confidence to embrace and welcome the changes I experienced as I matured. I'm grateful my early family experiences supported my efforts to live life as my true self, even as my life evolved.

Individuals raised in families without sufficient parental acceptance often struggle when their families shun them because their gender or sexuality are on the margins of society. As a result, many LGBTQIA+ persons feel they are "exiles from kinship,"[2] to use the words of Kate Weston, and need to form their own non-biological "families of choice" who support and accept them, serving as their attachment figures. Other individuals without family support may turn to relationships with God or a Higher Power to compensate for the rejection or loss they feel from their families. God becomes a substitute attachment figure and a safe haven because their human attachment relationships are inadequate.[3]

Reflecting on my life, I realize I was blessed to have a secure attachment with my religious parents. However, they were not perfect (no parents are) or without their deficits, and our relational interactions were sometimes challenging. At times, I felt Dad did not want to hear how I was developing different religious views because he wanted me to agree with him. Sometimes, I felt Mom was critical of me and paid too much attention to appearances. She was occasionally too concerned with what others would think and wanted us all to present Dad in his best light. There were days when I felt my parents didn't understand who I was becoming, especially in my late adolescence. However, I never doubted my parents' love and availability when I needed them to be my safe haven. Attachment research suggests that people who have an internal model of secure attachment and religious parents tend to view God as their supportive attachment figure and tend to be spiritual as well.[4] These research findings seem to fit my own life story.

The circle of security is an attachment concept that has been useful for me to understand my sense of self and my faith. The importance of my faith has ebbed and flowed over the decades. There were times when I felt a strong presence of the Holy Spirit, such as when I was at St. Mark's after my divorce. Sometimes, this feeling of the Holy Spirit was less prominent because I felt secure enough to explore the world; life events, such as graduate school and work, took priority. At other times, my doubts took precedence over my faith. At the beginning of the COVID pandemic, my faith was temporarily overwhelmed with doubts, like the doubts I experienced when I divorced and when my parents died. Yet those periods of doubt and grief led me back around to a sense that the Spirit was always with me, supporting me, holding me, and serving as my safe haven. Inevitably, I felt secure once more. In other words, my faith in God and the Holy Spirit is not linear, and the concept of the circle of security better captures the circular dynamics of my spiritual faith.

Reflecting on the metaphor of the circle of security has given me clarity and deeper insight into the fluid nature of my faith and my life journey. This metaphor is akin to the words of clinical psychologist James Finley of the Living School. In his memoir, *The Healing Path,* Finley has written about his childhood life of trauma and says that "from the hidden depths of darkness... God can emerge as a sovereign, silent presence that carries us forward."[5] He suggests that our spiritual journey through time has a "mysterious circular nature," which he further explains:

> *To be on the spiritual path is to know by experience how often the centrifugal force of our circular journey through time sends us flying out and away from our felt sense of interconnectedness with God's presence in our lives.... [but] we find our way back to the sense of God's sustaining presence, from which we had strayed in the immaturity and confusion of our wounded and wounding ways.*[6]

In the years ahead, I assume there will be changes in my spiritual life and biological health, leading to further changes in my faith and my sexuality. My aging will influence my faith as I contemplate life after bodily death and ponder resurrection beyond the spiritual resurrection I have experienced while alive on earth. As my body ages further, I will experience changes in my sexual desire and expression due to the normal physical and hormonal changes of old age. In other words, just as human development from early childhood through middle age influenced my faith and sexuality, late adulthood and aging itself continue to affect my faith and sexuality. My faith, sexuality, *and* aging are dynamic processes that are intertwined, evolving, and ever-changing.

One of the joys of late adulthood is that I have perspective and can reminisce, recall life transitions, and appreciate how memories of my life come together to form a picture of who I am. My faith journey has been a continual circle of security, always returning me to the safe haven of "the sense of God's sustaining presence."[7] I am grateful I continue to return to my early childhood belief in God's love. This simple message deeply rooted a trust in me that "God loves me just as I am." With this message in my heart, I have faith that God's presence will sustain me in the years to come.

C. SUSANNE BENNETT

Closing Reflection

Above all, trust in the slow work of God.
We are quite naturally impatient in everything to reach the
end without delay.
We should like to skip the intermediate stages.
We are impatient of being on the way to something unknown,
something new.

And yet it is the law of all progress
that it is made by passing through some stages of instability—
and that it may take a very long time.

And so I think it is with you;
your ideas mature gradually—let them grow,
let them shape themselves, without undue haste.
Don't try to force them on,
as though you could be today what time
(that is to say, grace and circumstances acting on your own
good will)
will make of you tomorrow.

Only God could say what this new spirit
gradually forming within you will be.
Give Our Lord the benefit of believing
that his hand is leading you,
and accept the anxiety of feeling yourself
in suspense and incomplete.

—Teilhard de Chardin, P. (n.d.). *Patient trust.*

C. SUSANNE BENNETT

Questions for Reflection and Discussion

Chapter 1: Childhood Simplicity

- What were some of the questions and doubts you remember having as a child about your life or your world?
- What childhood memories, if any, do you have about going to church or about your religious education?
- How would you describe your relationship with your parents, siblings, or caregivers as a young child?

Chapter 2: High School Questions

- When you became an adolescent, what doubts and questions did you have about your life, your religious beliefs, or what you had learned when you were younger?
- What do you recall about the first sexual or romantic feelings you had as an adolescent and how you acted on them? How do you feel about that now?
- What do you recall about your hopes and dreams about your future life after high school graduation?

Chapter 3: College Complexity

- After high school, how did you transition into young adulthood?
- What do you recall questioning or doubting when you were a young adult?
- How did you separate from your family regarding your behavior, beliefs, and values?
- What do you recall about your sexual attractions, views about sex and marriage, and views about sexual orientation and gender when you were a late teen or young adult?

Chapter 4: Marriage and Divorce

- How has your marriage or long-term relationship changed since it began?
- In a committed relationship, how have you and your partner been surprised and affected by secrets the two of you have later revealed to each other?
- When you are faced with a lack of intimacy in your relationship, how have you managed that void?
- If you have gone through a divorce, how did you manage the relationship's ending?

Chapter 5: Despair, Perplexity, New Life

- If you have been in a long-term relationship that ended in divorce or separation, how were you affected physically, emotionally, and spiritually?
- When you have felt most lonely, what helped you transition from that place?
- When you felt yourself in a tunnel of unknowing, what doubts and questions did you have?
- When you have felt in a stage of perplexity, how have you experienced the Divine?

Chapter 6: Changing Sexuality

- If you have been in a relationship that began in infatuation, how did it change over time?
- If you have been in a relationship where you felt emotionally abused, how did you respond?
- If you identify as straight, how do you imagine you would you feel being sexual with someone of the same sex?
- If you identify as gay, what was your own coming-out experience like?
- If you have experienced the death of a parent, how did you experience your grief?

Chapter 7: Graduate Education Perplexity

- How do you understand the origins of sexual orientation?
- How do you understand "sexual fluidity"?
- If you have been gay all your life, how do you understand transitioning later in life?
- When have you felt a sense of doubt or uncertainty about sexuality, faith, or your life?
- When have you ever been in a dark tunnel of unknowing and confusion about your life?

Chapter 8: New Marital Commitment

- What characteristics or traits draw you to another person in a relationship?
- How do you negotiate differences and disagreements in your romantic relationships?
- As your life has changed due to aging, how do you know you are with the person who best fits your life at your current developmental stage?

Chapter 9: Vocational Commitment

- What experiences in your work life have created challenges, such as feeling excluded because of your sexuality, faith, or other conflicts with colleagues, supervisors, or bosses?

- How did you manage these differences and difficulties?
- If you are retired, how did you know when it was time for you to retire from full-time employment?

Chapter 10: Retirement Harmony

- How do you feel about your retirement life if you have retired?
- How were you affected physically, emotionally, and spiritually by the COVID-19 pandemic?
- How do you feel about the growing racial, sexual, gender, and political discord in the world?
- If you sometimes feel on the margins of society because of your difference from the accepted and preferred "norms" of the majority, how do you manage your marginality?
- How do you make contributions to the world at this stage in your life?
- How do you experience God or a Divine Presence in your life today?

Author's Note

Social and gender terminology is constantly changing. I have chosen to use the terms that individuals in this book currently use to self-identify—*lesbian, gay, bisexual, trans, nonbinary, cis-gendered,* and *straight.* See the GLAAD website for an extensive definition of these terms.[1] The acronym *LGBTQIA+* stands for the community of Lesbian, Gay, Bisexual, Transgender, Queer/Questioning, Intersex, and Asexual individuals. The + stands for additional identities not listed in the acronym, and the term *straight* references the majority of individuals who do not self-identify as *LGBTQIA+.* Occasionally, more outdated terms— *heterosexuality* and *homosexuality*—are used when appropriate. *Nonbinary* is used to identify gender, meaning gender is neutral or does not fit into the either-or categories of male or female. In this book, the term *nonbinary* also refers to states or categories other than gender that are not defined as either-or. I recognize that a growing number of *LGBTQIA+* individuals self-identify as *queer,* but that was not the case in this story. The terms *white, Black, Indigenous,*

Latina, and *Filipino* refer to individuals in this memoir who self-identified with these terms for their racial identities. In this text, *Black, Indigenous, Latina,* and *Filipino* are capitalized to honor their cultural and historical significance, while *white* is left lowercase to reflect its position as a socially constructed default. Finally, the names and identifying details of most individuals in this memoir have been changed to protect their privacy, but my stories and the events are as true as I can remember them today.

Notes

Introduction: Stages and Themes

1. McLaren, B. (2021). *Faith after doubt: Why your faith stops working and what to do about it.* New York, NY: St. Martin's Publishing Group.

2. McLaren, p. 42.

3. Diamond, L. (2008). *Sexual fluidity: Understanding women's love and desire.* Cambridge, MA: Harvard University Press, p. 15.

4. Diamond, p. 3.

Chapter 1: Childhood Simplicity

1. Morrison, T. (2011, May 15). *Commencement address: Rutgers University, Class of 2011.* New York, NY: Rutgers University.

2. Battle of Hayes Pond. en.wikipedia.org/wiki/Battle_of_Hayes_Pond#cite_note-FOOTNOTEOakley200869-38

3. Lee, H. (1960). *To kill a mockingbird.* Philadelphia, PA: Lippincott.

4. McLaren, B. (2021).

5. McLaren, p. 46.

6. McLaren, p. xi.

Chapter 2: High School Questions

1. Rohr, R. (2011). *Falling upward: Spirituality for the two halves of life.* San Francisco, CA: Jossey-Bass. p. 5.

2. Dante Alighieri, 1265-1321. (1935). *The divine comedy of Dante Alighieri: Inferno, Purgatory, Paradise.* New York, NY: The Union Library Association.

3. Smith, H. (2009). *The religions of man.* New York, NY: Harpers One.

4. Frankl, V. E. (2006). *Man's search for meaning: An introduction to logotherapy.* Boston, MA: Beacon Press. (English translation 1959. Originally published in 1946 as *Ein Psychologe erlebt das Konzentrationslager,* "A Psychologist Experiences the Concentration Camp")

5. Gouwens, T. (1930). *Why I believe.* Cokesbury Press.

Chapter 3: College Complexity

1. Chittister, J., & Williams, R. (2014). *Uncommon gratitude: Alleluia for all that is.* Collegeville, MN: Liturgical Press, p. 15.

2. Kierkegaard, S. (1854). *Fear and trembling.* Translated from German by Walter Lowria. Garden City, NY: Doubleday and Company, p. 64.

3. Tillich, P. (1957). *Dynamics of faith.* New York, NY: Harper and Row Publishers.

4. Neitzsche, F. (1883-1892). *Thus spoke Zarathustra,* trans. Walter Kaufmann. New York, NY: Random House. 1954.

5. Vahanian, G. (1961). *The death of God.* George Braziller.

6. Tillich, P. (1952). *The courage to be.* New Haven, CT: Yale University Press, p.190.

Chapter 4: Marriage and Divorce

1. Chittister, J. (2023, Feb. 1). *Seeing it through.* Cornerstone of Hope. cornerstoneofhope.org/seeing-it-through

2. Goffman, E. (1963). *Stigma: Notes on the management of spoiled identity.* New York, NY: Simon & Schuster, Inc.

Chapter 5: Despair, Perplexity, New Life

1. Rohr, R. (2024, August 25). *Order, disorder, reorder.* Daily meditations, Sunday, August 25, 2024. Albuquerque, NM: Center for Action and Contemplation.

2. McLaren, p. 63.

Chapter 6: Changing Sexuality

1. Lorde, A. (n.d.). AZQuotes.com. Retrieved August 31, 2024, from AZQuotes.com Website: azquotes.com/quote/1169185

2. O'Donohue, J. (2008). For grief. *To bless the space between us.* New York, NY: Penguin Random House, p.117.

Chapter 7: Graduate School Perplexity

1. Hall, C. (2024). *Queering contemplation: Finding queerness in the roots and future of contemplative spirituality.* Minneapolis, MN: Broadleaf Books, p. 30.

2. Winnicott, D. (1965). *The maturational process and the facilitating environment: Studies in the theory of emotional development.* London: The Hogarth Press and the Institute of Psycho-Analysis.

3. Merton, T. (1961/2007). *New seeds of contemplation.* Abbey of Gethsemani, Inc. New York, NY: New Directions Publishing Corporation.

4. Rohr, R. (2011). *Falling upward: A spirituality for the two halves of life.* San Francisco, CA: Jossey-Bass.

5. Patterson, C. J. (1994). Children of the lesbian baby boom: Behavioral adjustment, self-concepts, and sex role identity. In B. Greene & G.M. Herek (Eds.). *Lesbian and gay psychology: Theory, research, and clinical applications* (pp. 156-175). Sage Publications.

6. Benkov, L. (1994). *Reinventing the family: Lesbian and gay parents.* New York, NY: Crown Paperbacks.

7. Cassidy, J. (1999). The nature of the child's ties. In J. Cassidy & P. Shaver (Eds.), *Handbook of attachment: Theory, research,*

and clinical applications (pp. 3–20). New York, NY: Guilford.

8. Bennett, S. (2003). Is there a primary mom? Parental perceptions of attachment bond hierarchies within lesbian adoptive families. *Child and Adolescent Social Work Journal, 20*(3), 159-173.

9. McLaren, p. 75.

10. Diamond, L., (2008), p. 3.

Chapter 8: New Marital Commitment

1. O'Donohue, J. (2008). For a new beginning. *To bless the space between us.* New York, NY: Penguin Random House, p. 14.

2. Brackett, J. (1875). *Simple Gift.* American Shaker Hymn. In the public domain.

Chapter 9: Vocational Commitment

1. O'Donohue, J. (2008). For a new position. *To bless the space between us.* New York, NY: Penguin Random House, p. 21.

2. Marvin, R., Cooper, G., Hoffman, K., & Powell, B. (2002). The circle of security project: Attachment-based intervention with caregiver-pre-school child dyads. *Attachment & Human Development, 4*(1), 107-124.

3. The Circle of Security® Network (2013). circleofsecuritynetwork.org/the_circle_of_security.html

4. Powell, B., Cooper, G., Hoffman, K., & Marvin, B. (2014). *The circle of security intervention: Enhancing attachment in early parent-child relationships.* New York, NY: The Guilford Press.

5. Bennett, S., & Nelson, J. (Eds.). (2010). *Adult attachment in clinical social work: Practice, research, and policy.* New York, NY: Springer Publishing. ISBN 978-1-4419-6240-9 DOI 10.1007/978-1-4419-6241-6

6. Bennett, S. (2010). Cultural relevance and bridging the divide: Teaching human behavior in conflict-affected Mindanao. *Reflections: Narratives of Professional Helping, 16*(4), 5-18.

7. Community and Family Services International. https://cfsi.ph

8. Bennett, S., & Rizzuto, C. (2011). Finding common ground: The perils of sameness and difference in the treatment of lesbian, gay, and bisexual clients. In J. Berzoff (Ed.), *Falling through the cracks: Psychodynamically oriented practice with vulnerable, oppressed, and at risk populations* (pp. 206-240). New York, NY: Jason Aronson.

9. Hall, p. 41.

10. McLaren, p. 101.

11. McLaren, p. 98.

Chapter 10: Retirement Harmony

1. O'Donohue, J. (2008). For retirement. *To bless the space between us*. New York, NY: Penguin Random House, p. 167.

2. Coates, T. (2019*). The water dancer: A novel*. New York, NY: One World.

3. Sacred Ground: A film-based dialogue series on race & faith. episcopalchurch.org/sacred-ground/

4. Thurman, H. (1949/2022). *Jesus and the disinherited*. Boston: Beacon Press.

5. Braveman, P., Akin, E., Protor, D., Kauh, T., & Holm, N. (2002). Systemic and structural racism: Definitions, examples, health damages, and approaches to dismantling. *Health Affairs, 41*(2). healthaffairs.org/doi/pdf/10.1377/hlthaff.2021.01394

6. Thurman, H., p. 4.

7. Cuch, F. (2020-21). *Native voices: Speaking to the church and the world*. Produced by Indigenous Ministries Office of The Episcopal Church.

8. Center for Action and Contemplation. cac.org/living-school/

9. Stillpoint. stillpointca.org/

10. McLaren, p. 101.

11. McLaren, p. 170.

12. McLaren, p. 100.

Epilogue: My True Self

1. Rohr, R. (2011). *Falling upward: A spirituality for the two halves of life.* San Francisco, CA: Jossey-Bass, p. 209.

2. Weston, K. (1991). *Families we choose: Lesbians, gays, kinship.* New York, NY: Columbia University Press.

3. Kirkpatrick, L. (2005). *Attachment, evolution, and the psychology of religion.* New York, NY: Guilford Press.

4. Kirkpatrick, L. (2005).

5. Finley, J. (2023). *The healing path: A memoir and an invitation.* Maryknoll, NY: Orbis Books, p. 28.

6. Finley, J., pp. 126-127.

7. Finley, J., p. 27

Author's Note

1. GLAAD website: glaad.org/reference/terms

Acknowledgements

I was delighted when my daughter gave me Storyworth as a Christmas gift two years ago. When I began responding to her weekly questions, I quickly realized how much I was engrossed in writing memories about my past. I am so grateful to my daughter for setting me on this writing path. Without her initial encouragement, I doubt this memoir would have been written.

I also deeply appreciate my wife for always being open and willing to listen to me with love when I read my writing aloud to her. She has read and heard every word of this book, often many times. I value her unwavering patience and honest input. Because she knows me better than anyone, I knew I could trust her to help me shape what to share with others.

Other family members, close friends, and colleagues read drafts of this book as it developed. Lallie, Margot, Marie, Laura, Barbara, Carlyle, Linda, Julie, Dan, Jeane, and Ralph–I thank you for the time you gave, your feedback, and your helpful suggestions, some of which I would not have considered without your perspective and wise advice.

I want to give further recognition and special acknowledgment to my Living School writing group. Thank you, Lallie, for creating a forum for Living School graduates to share writing with kindred spirits. Sharing spiritual writing with others on a similar spiritual journey has been a truly meaningful experience for me. I greatly appreciate how the core of this group—Lallie, Carol, Terrell, Mary, and Sherry—asked me challenging questions, encouraged me to deepen and expand my stories, and followed my progress over the last year. As you heard about my complicated life, you helped me feel safe to fill in the details, recall hidden memories, and risk being truthful with my readers. It was not always easy as a queer woman to share with five straight writers, but I am genuinely grateful for your prodding and your kind words of encouragement.

From this group, I want to express my particular gratitude to you, Sherry. I will be forever pleased that I contracted with you privately to help me "open up" my writing and add complexity to the story that I longed to share. I felt you understood me and envisioned the possibilities for this memoir. Your critiques were always given with warmth and sensitivity, encouraging me to continue this project and not give up, even when I sometimes felt discouraged. As someone who has successfully published a memoir, your knowledge about the publishing process opened my eyes to both the challenges and the possibilities.

I extend a final note of appreciation to Caitlin (and Mary, who referred you to me). As a professional editor and writer, you helped me move this memoir over the finish line. Your knowledge and expertise about the nonacademic publishing world have been invaluable. Without your services, this memoir would have remained unpublished on my computer. Your belief in my work and confidence that I have a worthy story helped me believe in myself and the value of publishing my memoir. Our commonalities regarding our spirituality and sexuality felt like the Holy Spirit brought us together—thank you God! And thank you, Caitlin.

About the Author

Dr. C. Susanne Bennett is a spiritual director, author, and educator. A retired psychotherapist and university professor, she has a PhD from Smith College in Massachusetts and a Master's in Social Work from The University of Maryland. She is the co-editor of *Adult Attachment in Clinical Social Work: Practice, Research, and Policy* and the author of numerous scholarly journal publications. Susanne completed the Center for Action and Contemplation's Living School in New Mexico and is an intern at Stillpoint's Art of Spiritual Direction in California. She resides on Cape Cod with her wife, providing spiritual direction, facilitating workshops, and volunteering for PFLAG-Cape Cod.

susannebennettphd.com